SPECTRUM®

Sight Words

Grade 1

Spectrum®
An imprint of Carson-Dellosa Publishing LLC
P.O. Box 35665
Greensboro, NC 27425 USA

Printed in the U.S.A. • All rights reserved. ISBN 978-0-7696-8211-2

05-028137784

Table of Contents

Table of Contents

Notes to Parents and Teachers

Whenever a young child reads, 50 to 75% of the words he or she comes across are from the Fry Instant Sight Word List. This is a highly respected, research-based list of the 300 most frequently used words in the English language. Typically, these high-frequency words do not follow regular phonics patterns or spelling rules, making them very difficult for young children to sound out or decode. Consequently, learning to recognize these words immediately "by sight" is a critical first step to successful, confident, fluent reading.

Spectrum Sight Words for First Grade, and its companion, *Spectrum Sight Words for Kindergarten*, introduce, practice, and review all of the words on this list to help children develop sight word mastery, confidence, and fluency as they encounter these words in both reading and writing. *Spectrum Sight Words* are intended for use in school programs or at home with 5-, 6-, and 7-year-olds. The contents are also suitable for older children needing more practice, or for younger children developing early reading skills.

Follow these helpful steps when using this book:
- Follow the exact sequence of the book's exercises, as each sight word is introduced—and then reviewed—in its specific order on the Fry Instant Sight Word List, beginning with the most frequently appearing words.
- Encourage your child to work at his or her own pace, and offer support and praise as he or she completes the exercises.
- Use the sight word flash card pages at the back of the book to create a set of flash cards for practice in reading and writing the sight words.
- Take advantage of the blank flash cards to personalize your child's flash card set.
- Review and evaluate sight word memory by having your child use the sight words in context, using the cloze sentence activities.
- Help your child develop and demonstrate sentence sense by using the scrambled sentence activities to reorganize sight words in correct sentence order.

As teachers and parents, it is our goal to support and foster the learning of all of our children. Activities and materials in *Spectrum Sight Words for First Grade* help meet those needs by promoting the appropriate pacing and challenge that allows each child to master reading success.

Target words: am, big, box

Directions: Write the words below. Say them as you write them.

```
    am              _____

    big             _____

    box             _____
```

Directions: Write the missing word in each sentence.

1. I _____ good at playing with my dog.

2. My dog is _____.

3. He is in a _____.

Now, write a sentence with these words in it: **big   box**

_____

_____

Target words: **ran, let, got**

Directions: Write the words below. Say them as you write them.

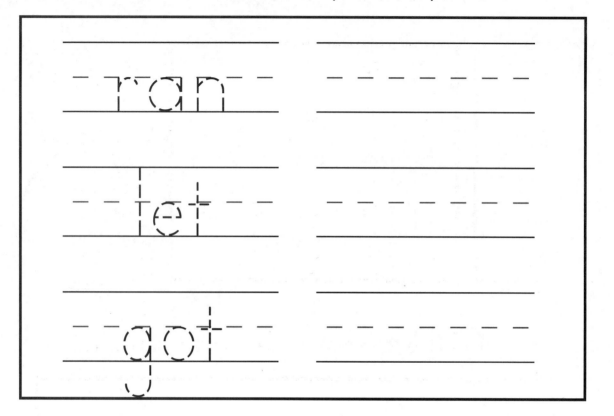

Directions: Write the missing word in each sentence.

1. I _____ a dog.

2. He _____ in the yard.

3. I _____ him lick me.

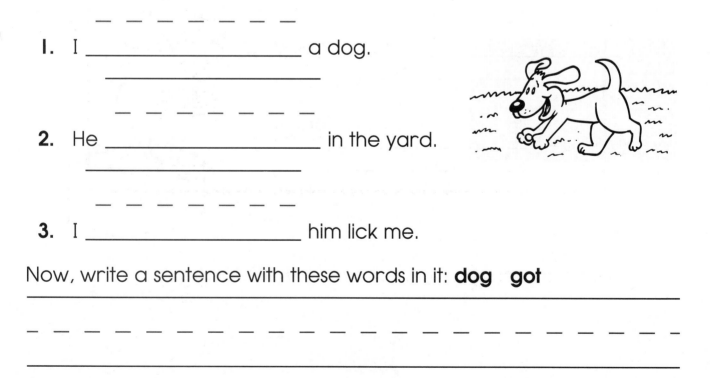

Now, write a sentence with these words in it: **dog   got**

_____

_____

Target words: am, big, box, ran, let, got

Directions: Find and circle the words from the box. Words can go →
or ↓.

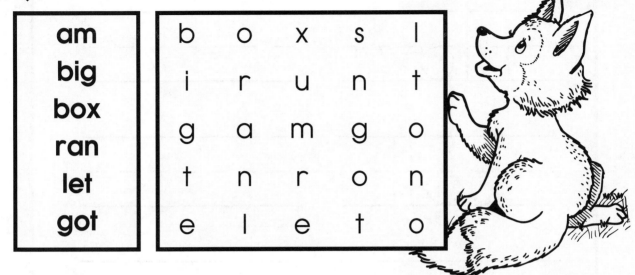

am
big
box
ran
let
got

b	o	x	s	l
i	r	u	n	t
g	a	m	g	o
t	n	r	o	n
e	l	e	t	o

Directions: Draw a line to connect the words that rhyme.

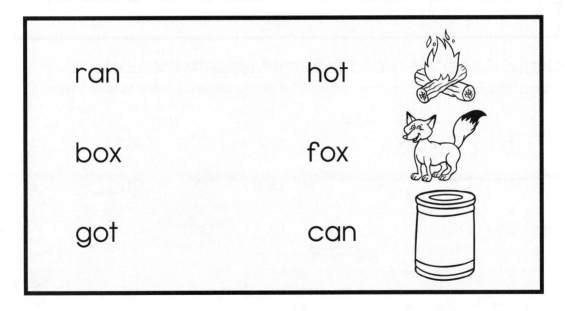

ran	hot
box	fox
got	can

Target words: play, ball, hat

Directions: Write the words below. Say them as you write them.

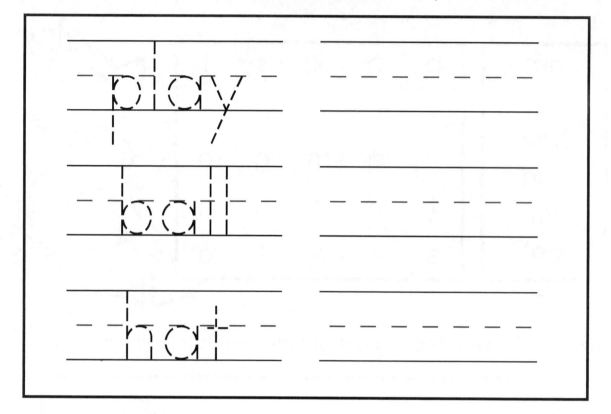

Directions: Circle the word that rhymes with the underlined word in each sentence.

1. The boy can <u>play</u>.   day   dog   pup

2. He has a <u>ball</u>.   bat   tall   bug

3. He has a <u>hat</u>.   hot   bat   ball

Target words: call, jump, sat

Directions: Write the words below. Say them as you write them.

c\-\-a\-l\-l\- \-\-\-\-\-\-\-\-\-

jump \-\-\-\-\-\-\-\-\-

sat \-\-\-\-\-\-\-\-\-

Directions: Write the missing word in each sentence.

1. The frog can _____.

2. He _____ by the pond.

3. I will not _____ to him.

4. _____ rhymes with **ball**.

Target words: play, ball, hat, call, jump, sat

Directions: Circle each set of footballs that have rhyming words on them.

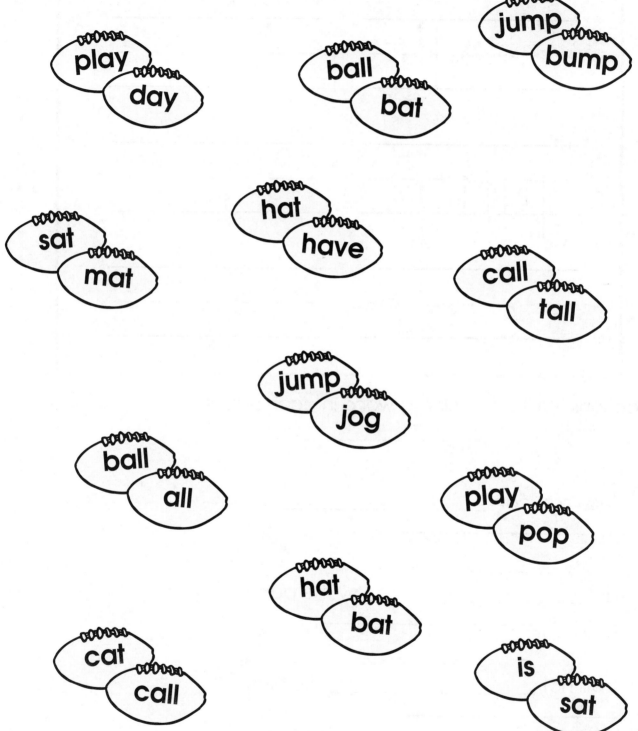

Target words: red, black, yellow, green

Directions: Write the words below. Say them as you write them.

red

black

yellow

green

Directions: Write the missing word in each sentence.

_____

_ _ _ _ _ _ _

1. A bear is _____.

_____

_ _ _ _ _ _ _

2. An apple is _____.

Target words: white, blue, brown, color

Directions: Write the words below. Say them as you write them.

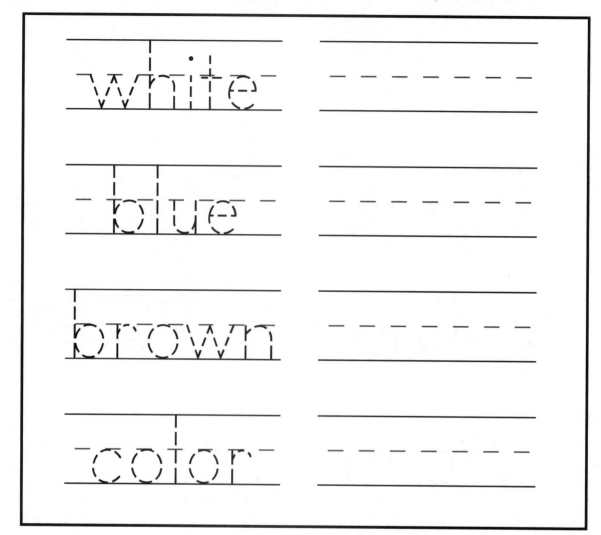

Directions: Write the missing word in each sentence.

white	blue	brown	color

1. I can color the bear _____.

2. The snowman is _____.

Target words: red, black, yellow, green, white, blue, brown, color

Directions:

1. Color bear number 1 blue.
2. Color bear number 2 green.
3. Color bear number 3 brown.
4. Color bear number 4 yellow.
5. Color bear number 5 white.
6. Color bear number 6 black.
7. Color bear number 7 red.

1

2

3

4

5

6

7

Target words: say, ask, friend

Directions: Write the words below. Say them as you write them.

Directions: The words **say, ask,** and **friend** are hiding in the lines below. Find and circle them. Now, color the boxes.

a	s	a	y	a	s	a	y	s	a	a	s	a	y	s	y

s	a	k	s	a	s	k	a	s	s	a	s	k	a	s	k

r	e	i	n	d	f	r	i	e	n	d	f	r	e	n	d

Target words: **way, may, today**

Directions: Write the words below. Say them as you write them.

way _____

may _____

today _____

Directions: Write the missing word in each sentence. Now, circle the words in each sentence that rhyme.

1. This is the _____ I want to play.

2. _____ I say this?

3. _____ is Monday.

Directions: Write 3 more words that rhyme with **way** and **may**.

_____ _____ _____

Target words: say, ask, friend, way, may, today

Directions: The letters in the words are mixed up. Unscramble them to write each word correctly. Use the words from the box to help you.

today	way	ask	say	friend

1. ksa

_____

2. yas

_____

3. drfeni

_____

4. doayt

_____

5. wya

_____

Directions: Unscramble the words in this sentence. Now, write the sentence.

I play with my drfeni.

_____

_____

Target words: girl, look, find

Directions: Write the words below. Say them as you write them.

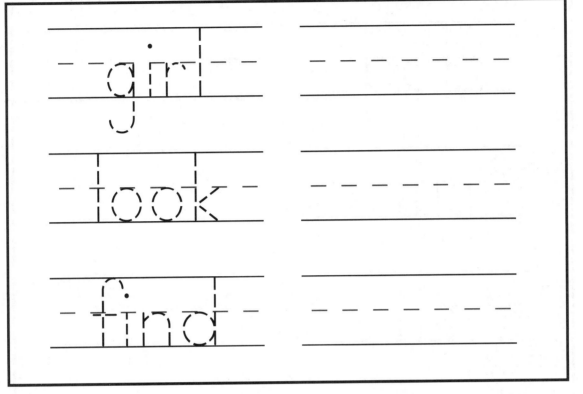

Directions:

1. Circle the box that says **look**.
2. Color the box that says **find**.
3. Put an **X** on the box that says **girl**.

girl   like   find

fun   look   boy

Directions: Circle the two words in each row that are the same.

love	look	like	look
find	four	five	find
girl	girl	got	goat

Target words: **dog, run, sit, yes**

Directions: Write the words below. Say them as you write them.

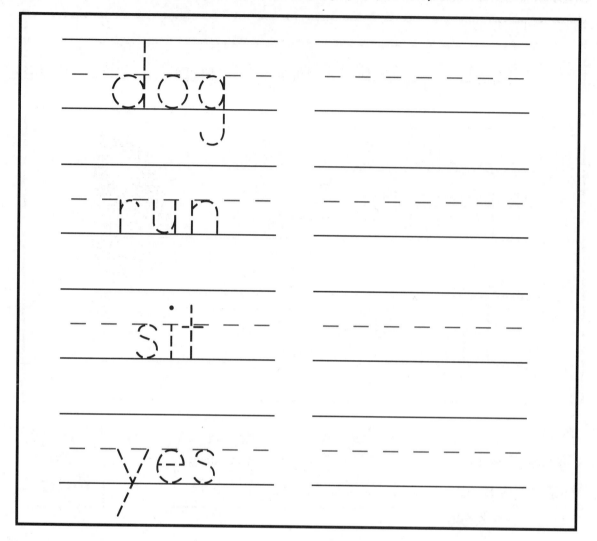

Directions: Find and circle the dog bones with the words from the box on them.

| dog | run | sit | yes |

How many did you circle? _____

girl, look, find, dog, run, sit, yes

. Use the words from the box to write the missing word in
ntence.

| girl | look | find | dog | run | sit | yes |

_____

– – – – – – –

1. A _____ had a dog.

_____

– – – – – – –

2. He liked to _____ fast.

_____

– – – – – – –

3. One day she lost her _____.

_____

– – – – – – –

4. She could not _____ him.

_____

– – – – – – –

5. She had to _____ for him. Did she find him?

_____

– – – – – – –

6. _____, she did.

_____

– – – – – – –

7. Now she wants him to _____.

Target words: four, five, six, seven, eight

Directions: Write the words below. Say them as you write them.

four

five

six

seven

eight

Directions: Draw a line to the number that matches the word.

six	4
four	8
five	6
seven	5
eight	7

Target words: **nine, ten, money, buy**

Directions: Write the words below. Say them as you write them.

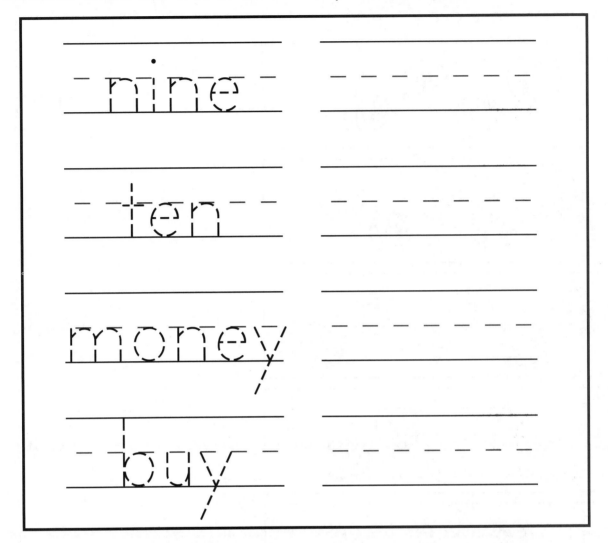

Directions: Write the missing word in each sentence. Then, write the answers.

_____

1. Can she _____ a pencil?

2. How much _____ does she have?

Target words: four, five, six, seven, eight, nine, ten, money, buy

Directions: Draw a line from each box to the word that tells how many coins there are.

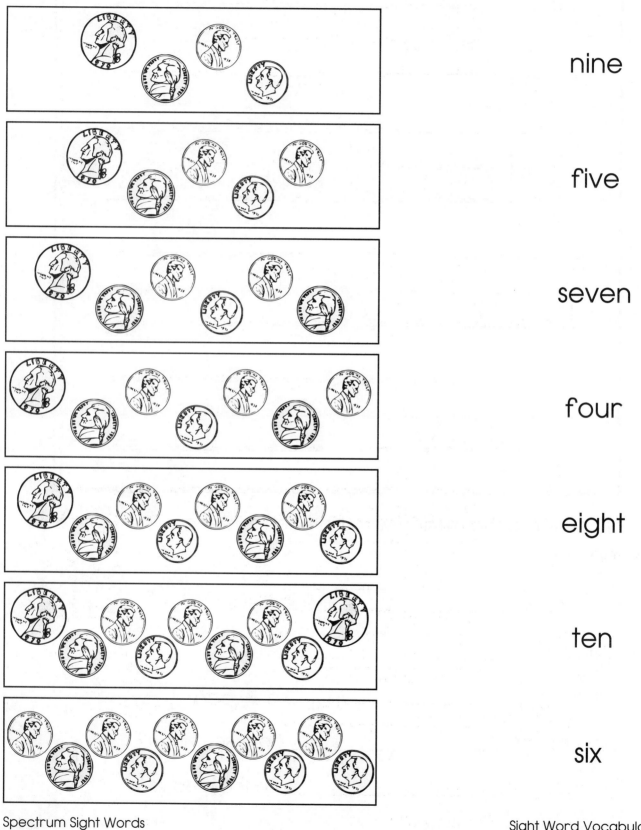

nine

five

seven

four

eight

ten

six

Sight Word Vocabulary

Target words: **under, upon, next, near**

Directions: Write the words below. Say them as you write them.

under   _ _ _ _ _ _ _

upon   _ _ _ _ _ _ _

next   _ _ _ _ _ _ _

near   _ _ _ _ _ _ _

Directions: Write the missing word in each sentence.

_ _ _ _ _ _ _

1. The rock is _____ a tree.

_ _ _ _ _ _ _

2. The frog sits _____ a lily pad.

_ _ _ _ _ _ _

3. The mouse is _____ to the elephant.

Target words: high, tree, found

Directions: Write the words below. Say them as you write them.

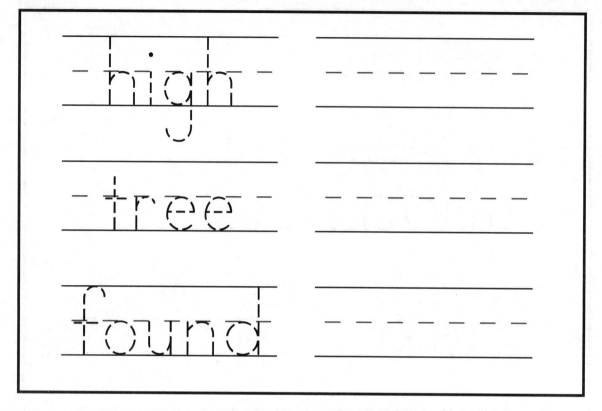

Directions: Unscramble the letters to make the words from the box.
Now, write the correct word next to each apple.

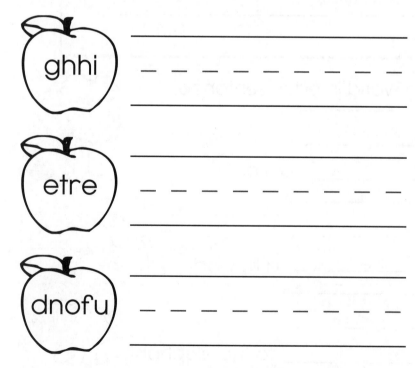

Target words: under, upon, next, near, high, tree, found

Directions: Read each sentence. Now, write it on the line.

The boy ran next to his dog.

_____

- -

_____

They sat upon a bench.

_____

- -

_____

A rock is under the tree.

_____

- -

_____

He threw it high up.

_____

- -

_____

He found it near the tree.

_____

- -

_____

Target words: until, into, same

Directions: Write the words below. Say them as you write them.

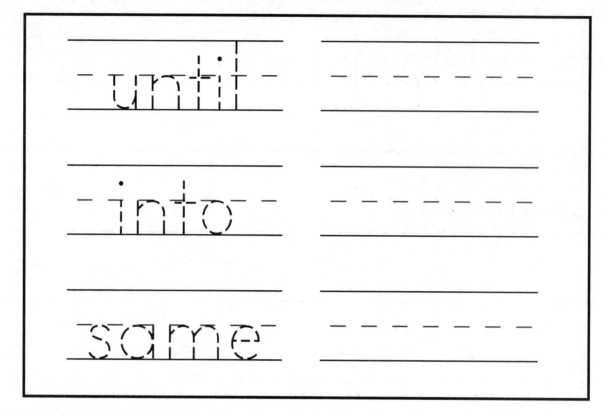

until

into

same

Directions: Color the apples that have the same words on them.

under
until

into
into

same
some

same
same

into
onto

until
until

Target words: hard, part, round

Directions: Write the words below. Say them as you write them.

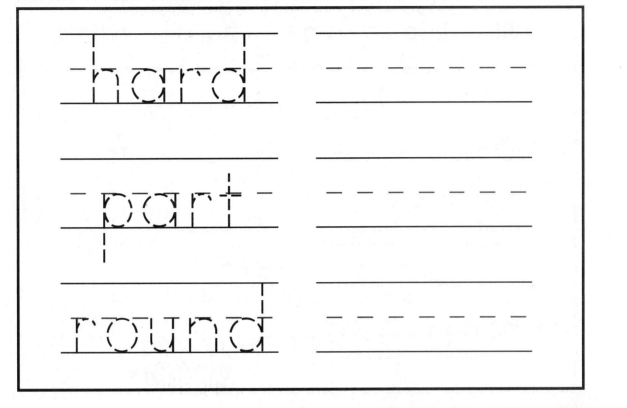

Directions: Draw a line to connect the bouncing balls to get to the basket. Use the words from the box.

round	hard
part	

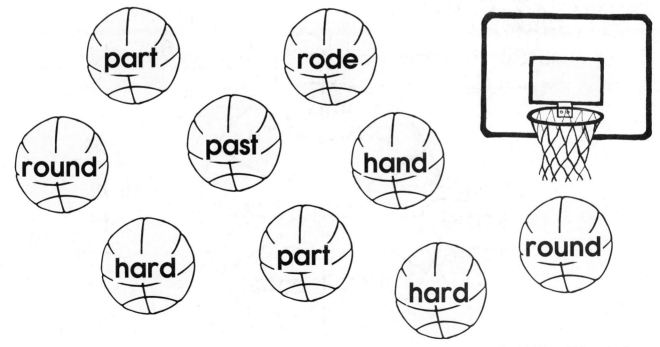

Target words: until, into, same, hard, part, round

Directions: Write the missing word in each sentence.

until	into	same	hard	round

_____
– – – – – – – – –

1. An apple is _____.

_____
– – – – – – – – –

2. It is _____.

_____
– – – – – – – – –

3. You can bite _____ it.

_____
– – – – – – – – –

4. Eat it all _____ it is gone.

_____
– – – – – – – –

5. The two parts are the _____.

Directions: Color the spaces that have words that rhyme with the word in the middle.

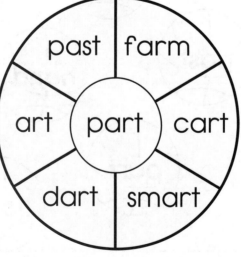

Target words: fat, funny, might

Directions: Write the words below. Say them as you write them.

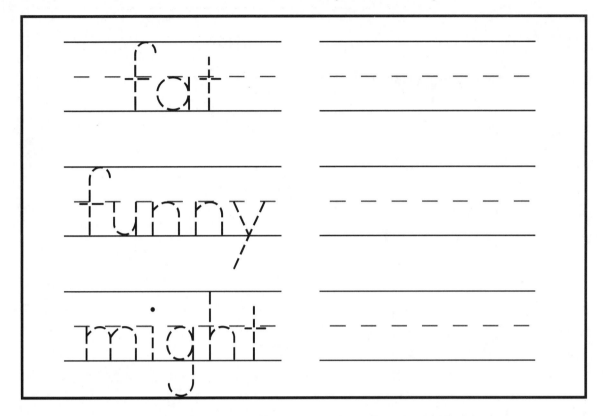

Directions: Draw a line to connect the words that rhyme.

fat   night

funny   bunny

might   cat

Now, draw a
fat, funny mouse.

Target words: saw, only, such, never

Directions: Write the words below. Say them as you write them.

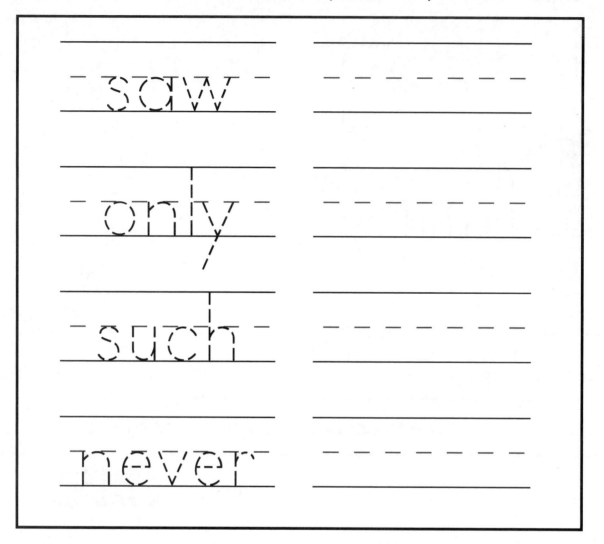

Directions: The words **saw**, **only**, **such**, and **never** are hiding in the boxes below. Find them and color the boxes that have these words in them.

one	only	on	only
saw	was	sun	saw
much	such	such	more
never	ever	never	even

Target words: fat, funny, might, saw, only, such, never

Directions: Find and circle the words from the box. Words can go →
or ↓.

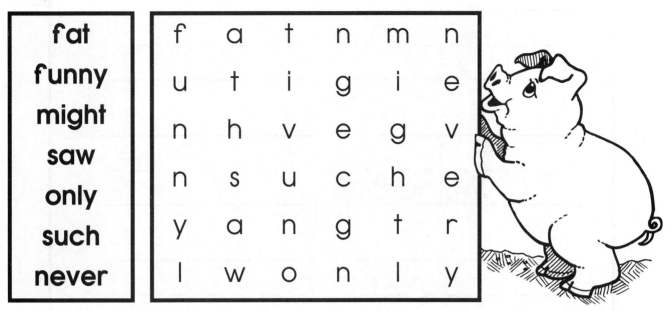

| fat |
| funny |
| might |
| saw |
| only |
| such |
| never |

f	a	t	n	m	n
u	t	i	g	i	e
n	h	v	e	g	v
n	s	u	c	h	e
y	a	n	g	t	r
l	w	o	n	l	y

Directions: Color the spaces that have words that rhyme with the
word in the middle of the circle.

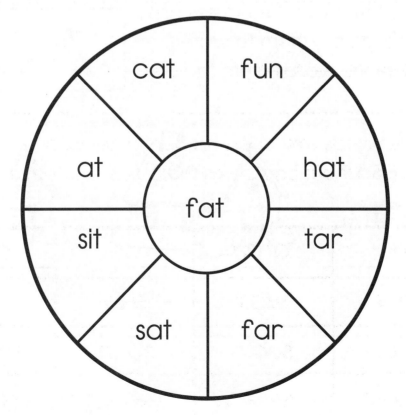

Target words: live, house, home

Directions: Write the words below. Say them as you write them.

live

house

home

Directions: The letters on the houses are mixed up. Unscramble them to write each word. Use the words from the box to help you.

live   house
home

ohues   emoh   evil

Target words: mother, sister, brother

Directions: Write the words below. Say them as you write them.

mother _____

sister _____

brother _____

Directions: Select the word from the box that answers these riddles.

| mother | sister | brother |

I am a girl. _____

I am a boy. _____

I am a woman. _____

Now, draw a picture of yourself.

Target words: live, house, home, mother, sister

Directions: Find and circle the words from the box. Words can go →
or ↓.

live

house

home

mother

sister

m	s	m	h	t	l
o	i	u	o	e	r
t	s	s	u	h	l
h	t	o	s	t	i
e	e	u	e	o	v
r	r	h	o	m	e

Directions: Draw a picture of where you live.

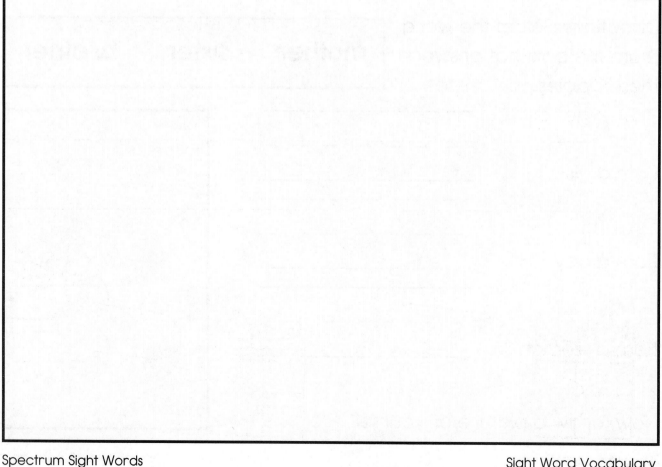

Target words: each, own, name

Directions: Write the words below. Say them as you write them.

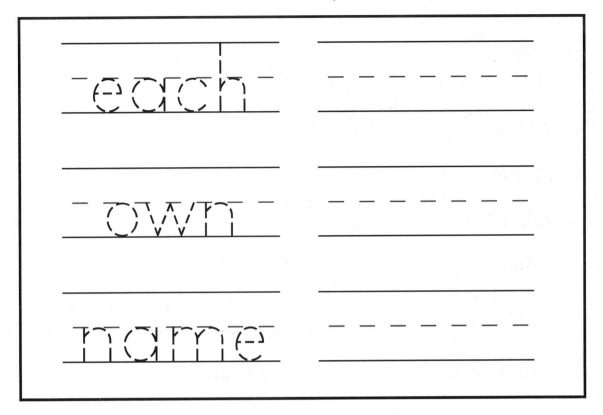

each _____

own _____

name _____

Directions: Read the sentences below and follow the directions.

1. Write your own name on each tag.
2. Color each present blue.
3. What do you think is in the boxes?

_____

_____

Target words: **year, also, fall**

Directions: Write the words below. Say them as you write them.

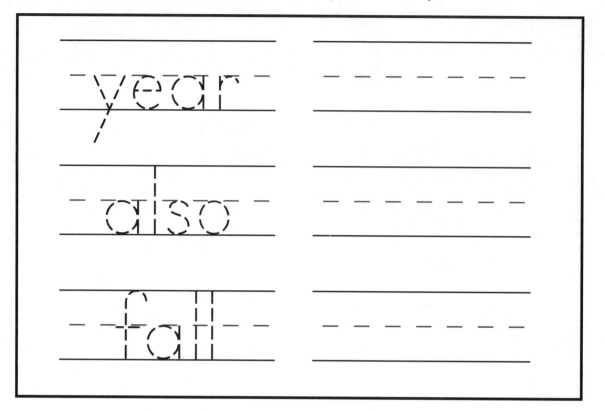

Directions: Read these sentences and draw a picture of them.

Every year the leaves fall.

I like to rake the leaves.

And I also like to jump in them.

Target words: each, own, name, year, also, fall

| each | own | name | year | also | fall |

Directions: Find the leaves that have the words from the box on them. Color them these colors:

each = red   **own** = green   **name** = yellow

year = orange   **also** = brown

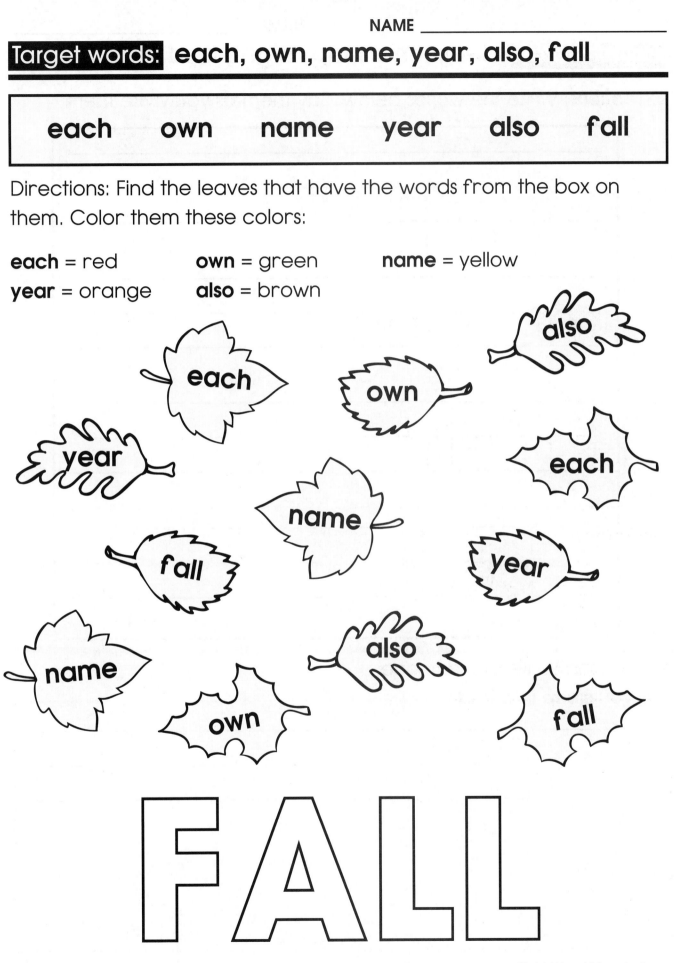

Target words: sleep, morning, night, bed

Directions: Write the words below. Say them as you write them.

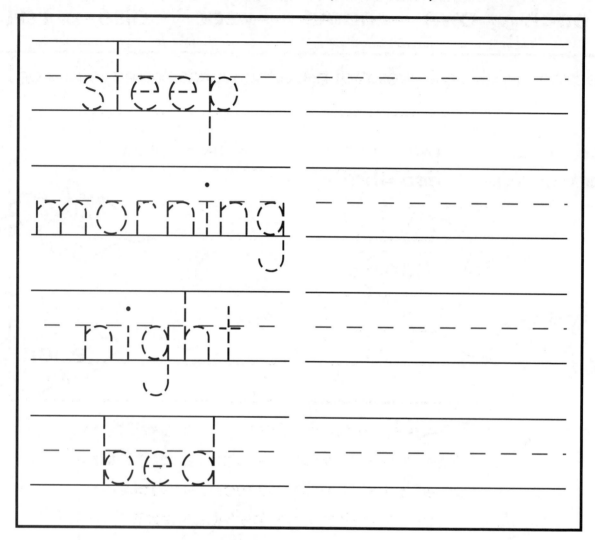

Directions: Write this sentence.

Do you sleep in a bed?

_____

- -

_____

Target words: o'clock, early, school

Directions: Write the words below. Say them as you write them.

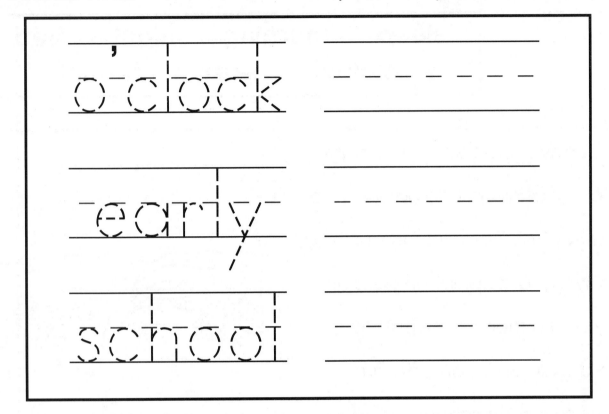

Directions: Read the sentences and follow the directions.

1. Write **one** under the star with the word **o'clock** on it.
2. Write **two** under the star with the word **school** on it.
3. Write **three** under the star with the word **early** on it.

Target words: sleep, morning, night, bed, o'clock, early, school

Directions: Read the story. Now, find and circle the words that are in the box.

sleep	**morning**	**night**	**bed**
	o'clock	**early**	**school**

I have to go to bed at eight

o'clock at night. I do not like to go

to sleep too early. In the morning,

I have to get up. When I get up,

my dog is there. He wants to go

on a walk. So I walk with him

before I go to school.

What time do you go to bed? Show it on the clock and write the time on the line.

_____

– – – – – – – – – – – – – – – – – – – –

_____

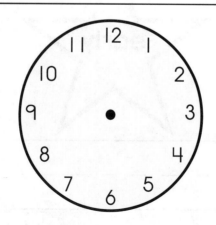

Target words: open, close, leave

Directions: Write the words below. Say them as you write them.

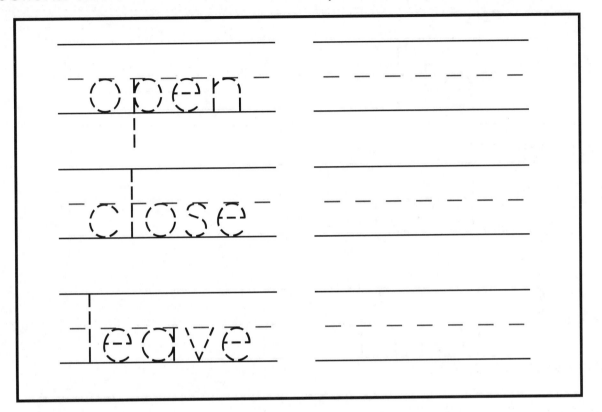

Directions: Draw a picture of each sentence.

I open the book.

I close the book.

I will leave the book on my bed.

Target words: off, door, don't

Directions: Write the words below. Say them as you write them.

Directions: Write the missing word in each sentence. Use the words from the box to help you.

| off | door | don't |

1. I will turn _____ the light.

2. _____ close the door.

3. The _____ is open.

Target words: open, close, leave, off, door, don't

Directions: Read the story. Now, find and circle the words from the box.

open	close	leave
off	door	don't

One night I had to leave the door open. I do not like the dark, so I said, "Mom, don't close the door." Then I said, "Don't turn the light off." Then I went to sleep.

Directions: Draw a line to connect words that are opposites.

on

open

do

don't

off

close

Target words: read, book, over

Directions: Write the words below. Say them as you write them.

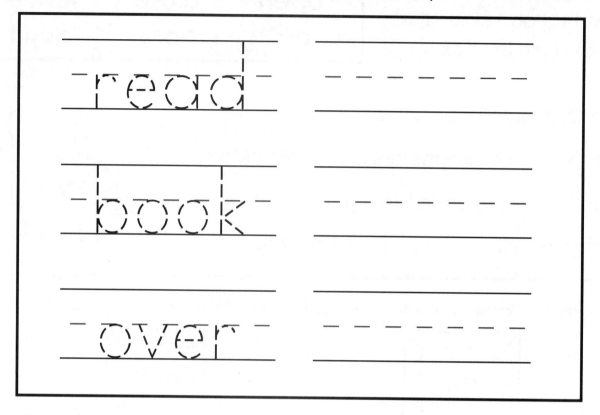

Directions: Several words below are mixed up. Unscramble the letters and write all the words on the lines. Use the words from the box.

book	over	read	and	can	I	a

I _____ nac _____ daer _____ a _____ kobo

_____ voer _____ dna _____ voer.

Target words: another, because

Directions: Write the words below. Say them as you write them.

another _ _ _ _ _ _ _

because _ _ _ _ _ _ _

Directions: Draw a picture for each sentence.

I want another dog.

I am hot because the sun is out.

I am cold because I lost my shoes.

Let's get another pumpkin.

Target words: read, book, over, another, because

Directions: Use the words from the box to complete the story.

read	book	over
another	because	

The girl is sitting in a chair. She likes to _____

_____

her _____ here. She will even

_____

read _____ book, too. She has lots of books

_____

_____ she likes to read. She will read her

_____

books _____ again.

Directions: Circle the books with the same words on them.

read
red

read
read

book
book

anything
another

book
look

over
over

Target words: car, far, ride, around

Directions: Write the words below. Say them as you write them.

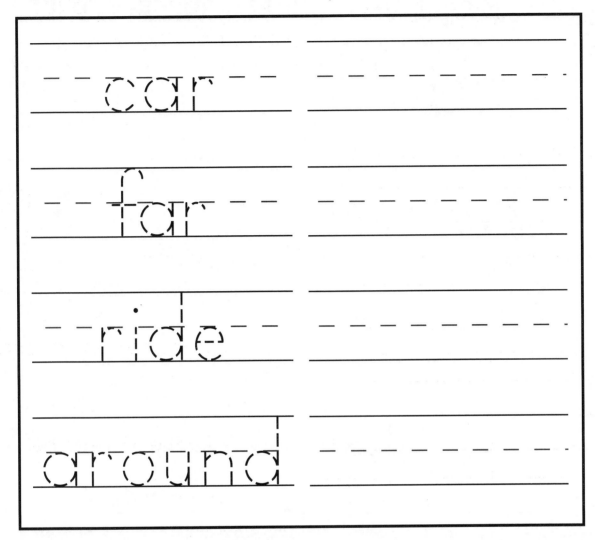

Directions: Color the cars that have words that rhyme with **ride**.

Target words: back, away, town, took

Directions: Write the words below. Say them as you write them.

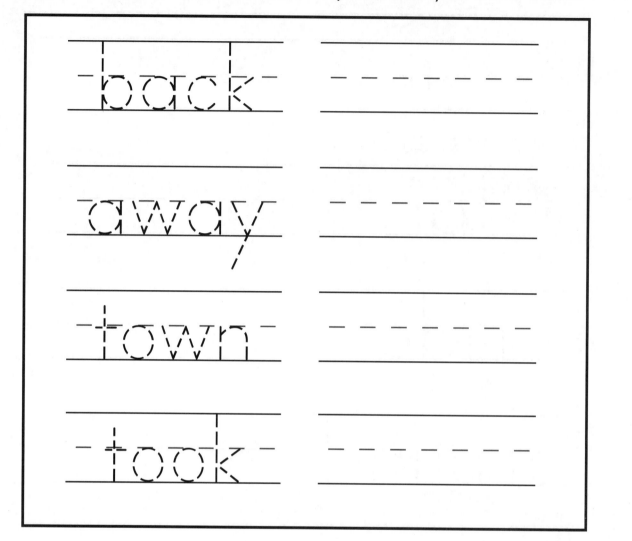

Directions: Read each sentence. Circle the
word that rhymes with the underlined word.

1.	The car went <u>back</u> home.	bag	sack	come
2.	Will the bug go <u>away</u>?	rug	till	stay
3.	We went all over <u>town</u>.	too	down	ball
4.	It took a <u>long</u> time to get home.	lot	look	song

NAME _____

Target words: car, far, ride, around, back, away, town, took

Directions: Find and circle the words from the box. Words can go →
or ↓.

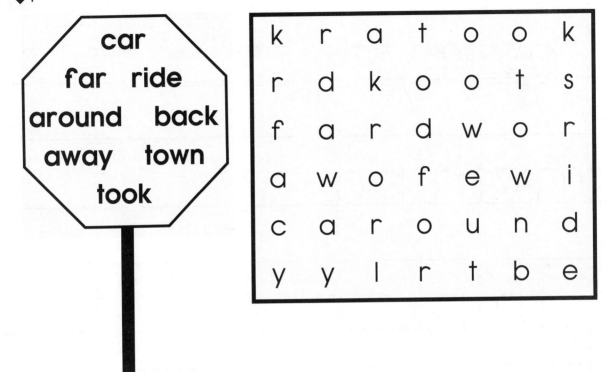

car
far ride
around back
away town
took

k	r	a	t	o	o	k
r	d	k	o	o	t	s
f	a	r	d	w	o	r
a	w	o	f	e	w	i
c	a	r	o	u	n	d
y	y	l	r	t	b	e

Directions: The words **town** and **ride** are hiding in the boxes below.
Find and circle them.

| w | n | t | o | w | n | t | o | n | w | o | t | o | w | n |

| e | d | r | i | d | e | r | i | d | r | i | d | e | e | d | e |

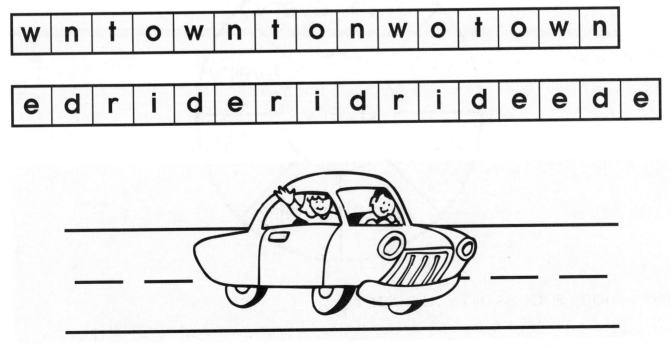

Target words: every, anything, think

Directions: Write the words below. Say them as you write them.

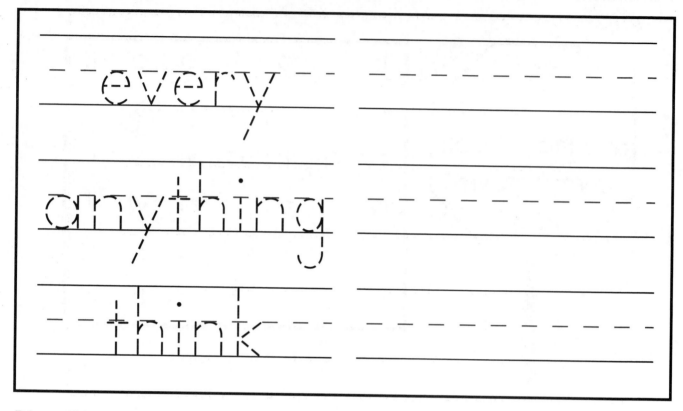

Directions: Color the spaces that have the same word as the one in the middle of the circle.

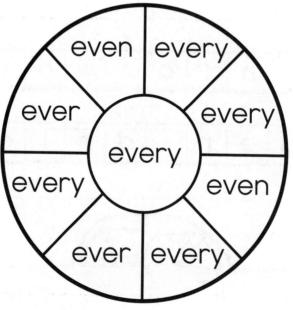

How many spaces did you color? _____

Target words: people, could, too

Directions: Write the words below. Say them as you write them.

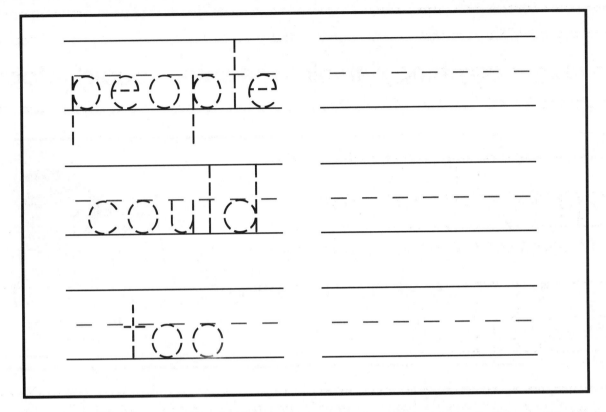

Directions: Unscramble the letters to make the words from the box.
Now, write them on the line under each book.

could	people	too

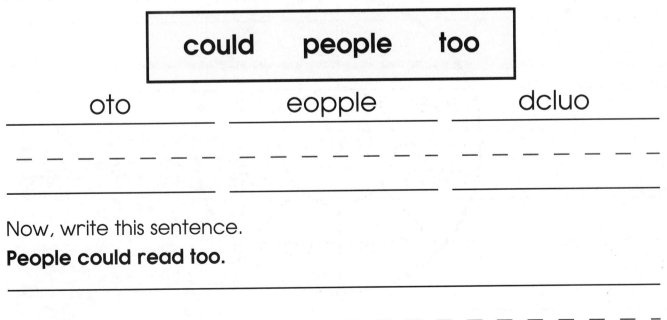

oto   eopple   dcluo

Now, write this sentence.

People could read too.

Target words: **every, anything, think, people, could, too**

Directions: Read the story. Now, find and circle the words from the box.

every	anything	think	people	could	too

I love to read every book I can.

I tell my friends that they could, too.

They could read as many books as I do.

I think lots of people could read anything

they want. Let's read!

Now, write a sentence telling what you think people would like to read about.

_____

- -

_____

_____

- -

_____

- -

_____

Target words: men, woman, along

Directions: Write the words below. Say them as you write them.

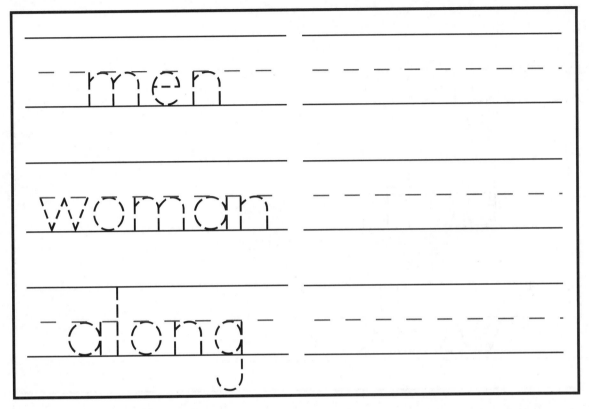

Directions: Color the spaces that have the same word as the one in the middle of the circle.

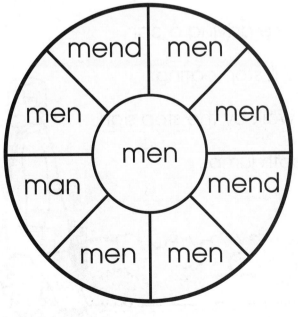

How many spaces did you color? _____

Target words: **stop, both, walk**

Directions: Write the words below. Say them as you write them.

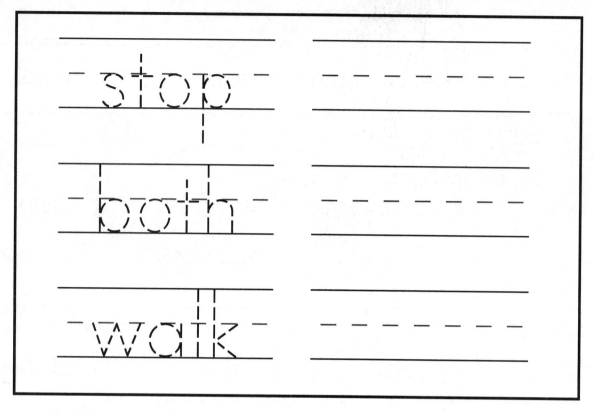

stop

both

walk

Directions: Look at the picture. Which sentence tells about the picture? Put an **X** by that sentence.

1. _____ Both men are driving a car.

2. _____ Both men will stop eating.

3. _____ Both men walk by the stop sign.

4. _____ The men both jump.

Target words: men, woman, along, stop, both, walk

Directions: To get to the street, draw a line to connect the stop signs that contain the words from the box. The first one is done for you.

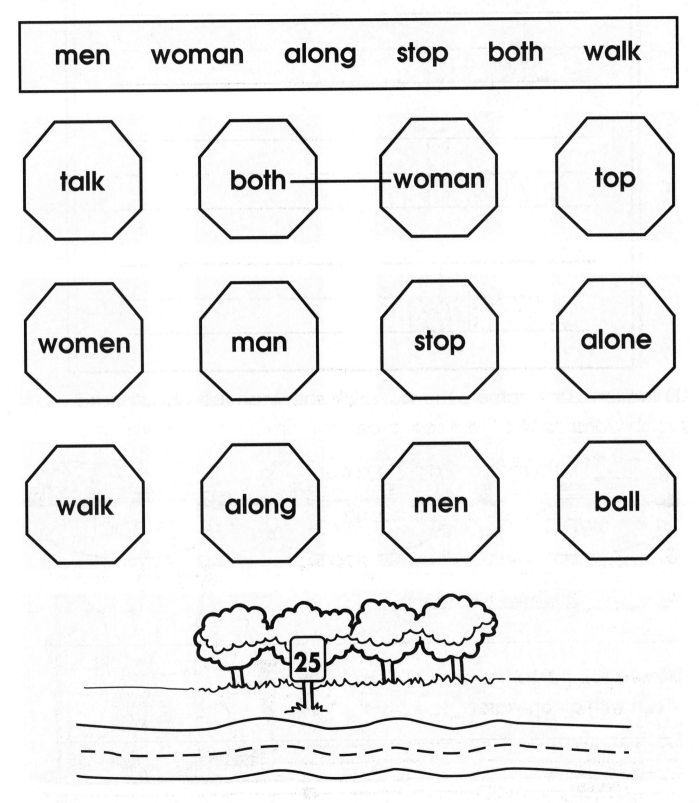

| men | woman | along | stop | both | walk |

Target words: clean, wash, water

Directions: Write the words below. Say them as you write them.

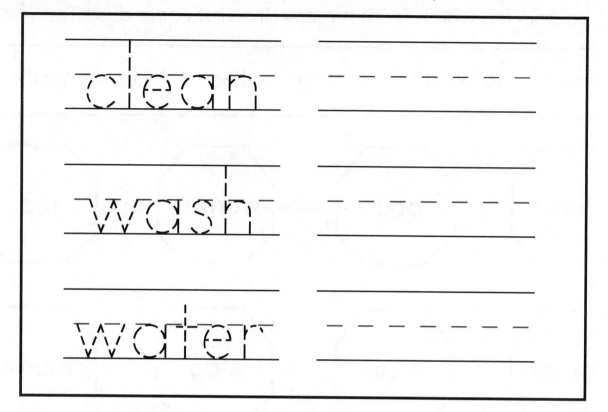

Directions: Unscramble the words on the wash tubs. Now, write each word on the line. Use the words from the box to help you.

swha   retwa   enacl

Now, write this sentence.

Wash with clean water.

Target words: carry, hot, warm

Directions: Write the words below. Say them as you write them.

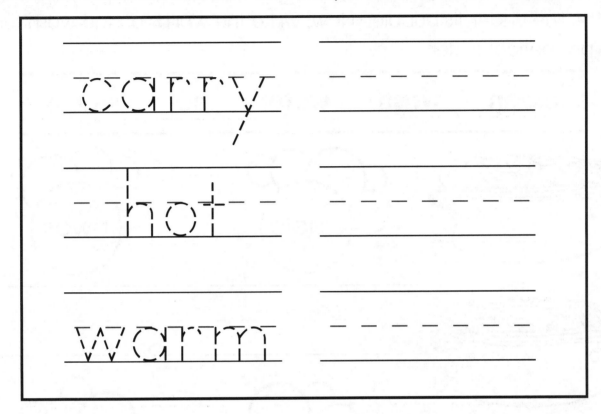

Directions: Draw a line from each bucket to its matching word.

carrot   carry   cart   carry

hot   hop   lot   hot

wash   what   water   water

Target words: clean, wash, water, hot, warm

Directions: Unscramble the words from the box. Write each word on the line under its bubble. Now, write the words on the wash tubs in alphabetical order.

| clean | wash | water | hot | warm |

Target words: clothes, coat, cold

Directions: Write the words below. Say them as you write them.

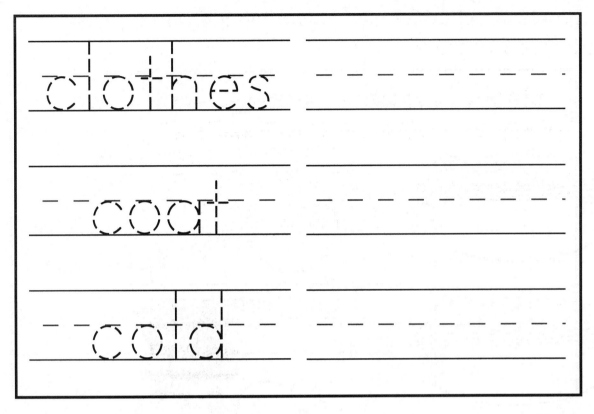

Directions: Color the spaces that have words that rhyme with the same word in the middle of the circle.

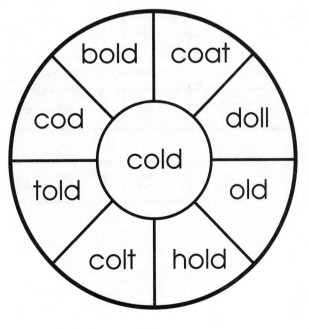

How many spaces did you color? _____

Target words: kind, dress, better

Directions: Write the words below. Say them as you write them.

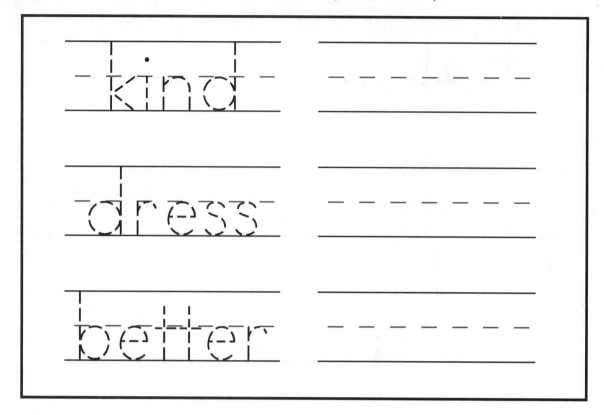

Directions: The words **kind**, **dress**, and **better** are hidden in the lines below. Find and circle them. Now, color the boxes.

| k | n | d | k | i | n | d | n | k | i | n | d | n | i | k | n |

| r | s | e | d | s | r | d | r | e | s | s | d | r | e | s | s |

| b | e | b | e | t | t | e | r | b | t | b | e | t | t | e | r |

Target words: clothes, coat, cold, kind, dress, better

Directions: Find and circle the words from the box. Words can go → or ↓.

clothes	coat	cold	kind	dress	better

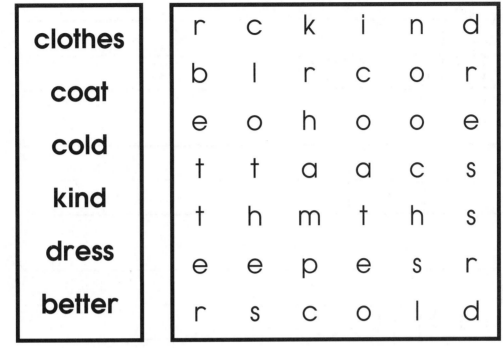

```
r  c  k  i  n  d
b  l  r  c  o  r
e  o  h  o  o  e
t  t  a  a  c  s
t  h  m  t  h  s
e  e  p  e  s  r
r  s  c  o  l  d
```

Directions: Draw a line to connect each word to its picture.

1. kind

2. coat

3. clothes

4. dress

5. cold

6. better

Target words: please, tell, once

Directions: Write the words below. Say them as you write them.

please   _____

tell   _____

once   _____

Directions: Write the missing word in each sentence. Use the words from the box to help you.

once	tell	please

_____

1. Will you _____ close the door?

2. I can _____ time.

3. _____, I fell in a lake.

Target words: use, made

Directions: Write the words below. Say them as you write them.

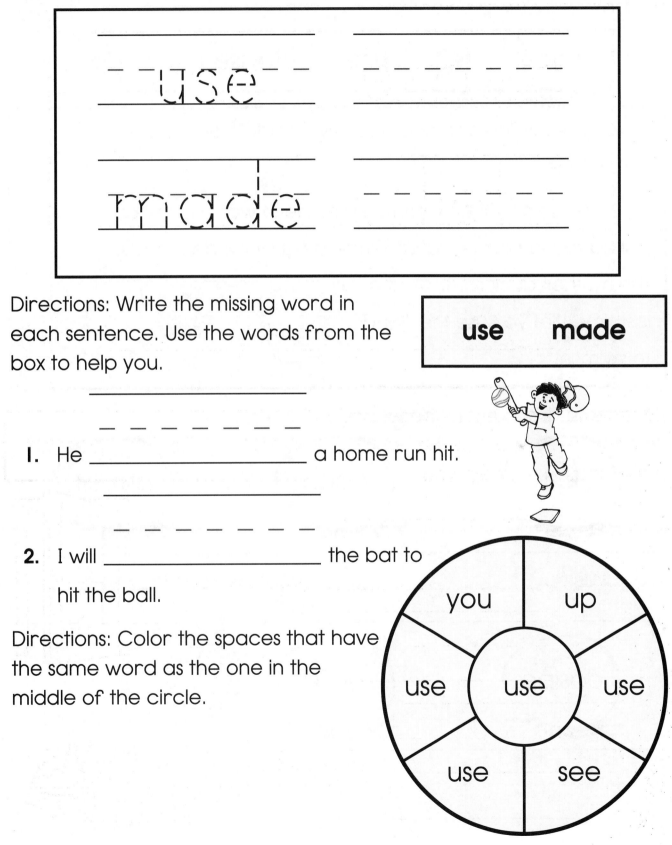

use

made

Directions: Write the missing word in each sentence. Use the words from the box to help you.

use	made

1. He _____ a home run hit.

2. I will _____ the bat to

    hit the ball.

Directions: Color the spaces that have the same word as the one in the middle of the circle.

you   up

use   use   use

use   see

Target words: please, tell, once, use, made

Directions: Read the story. Now, find and circle the words from the box.

once	tell	use	please	made

Once, I wanted to hear a story. I said, "Dad, please tell me one."

Dad said, "Once upon a time, there was a baby duck. It liked to play in the water. Once a day it made a mess. The mother duck said, "That is the last time I let you use the pond to swim in!"

Directions: Unscramble the words on the eggs.

letl

econ

emda

_____

_____

_____

_____

_____

_____

easlpe

seu

_____

_____

_____

_____

Target words: fly, fast, goes

Directions: Write the words below. Say them as you write them.

Directions: Color the spaces that have the same word as the one in the middle of the circle.

good | gone
goes | goes
goes
gone | good
goes | goes

Now, write this sentence.

A plane can fly fast.

Target words: try, though, why

Directions: Write the words below. Say them as you write them.

Directions: Write the missing word in each sentence. Use the words from the box to help you.

| try | though | why |

1. I _____ to tie my shoes.

2. It is hard to do it _____.

3. I don't know _____ it is hard to do.

Target words: fly, fast, goes, try, though, why

Directions: Find and circle the words from the box. Words can go →
or ↓.

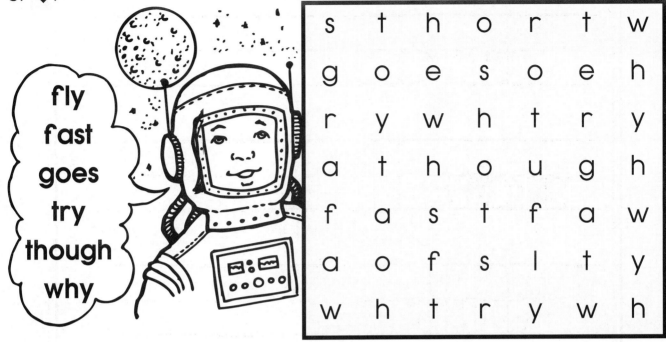

s	t	h	o	r	t	w
g	o	e	s	o	e	h
r	y	w	h	t	r	y
a	t	h	o	u	g	h
f	a	s	t	f	a	w
a	o	f	s	l	t	y
w	h	t	r	y	w	h

fly
fast
goes
try
though
why

Directions: Draw a line to connect the planes that have words that rhyme.

though

why

fly

try

fast

goes

Target words: **food, ate, full**

Directions: Write the words below. Say them as you write them.

food

ate

full

Directions: Write the missing word in each sentence.

food	ate	full

1. I like to eat _____.

2. If I eat too much, I get _____.

3. Last night, I _____ too much.

Target words: most, more, always

Directions: Write the words below. Say them as you write them.

most

more

always

Directions: Write the missing letters from the words below. Use the words from the box to help you.

| most | more | always |

1. mo ____ t

2. a ____ way ____

3. mo ____ e

Now, write a sentence using one of the words from the box.

_____

- - - - - - - - - - - - - - - - - - - -

_____

Target words: food, ate, full, most, more, always

Directions: Find and circle the words from the box. Words can go →
or ↓.

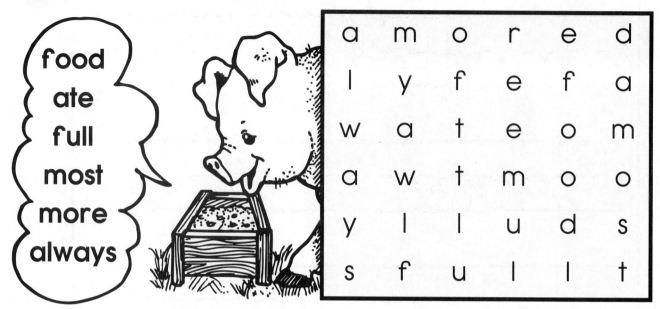

food
ate
full
most
more
always

a	m	o	r	e	d
l	y	f	e	f	a
w	a	t	e	o	m
a	w	t	m	o	o
y	l	l	u	d	s
s	f	u	l	l	t

Directions: Read the story. Now, find and circle the words from
the box.

This food is good. I always

eat too much. My dad eats the most.

One night he ate it all! Now he is

always full. He can not eat any more.

Target words: write, letter, dear, love

Directions: Write the words below. Say them as you write them.

Directions: Answer the questions below using the words from the box.

letter	dear

_____

- - - - - - - -

1. What do you send in the mail? _____

_____

- - - - - - - -

2. What word do you use to begin a letter? _____

Target words: write

Directions: Color the spaces that have the same word as the one in the middle of the circle.

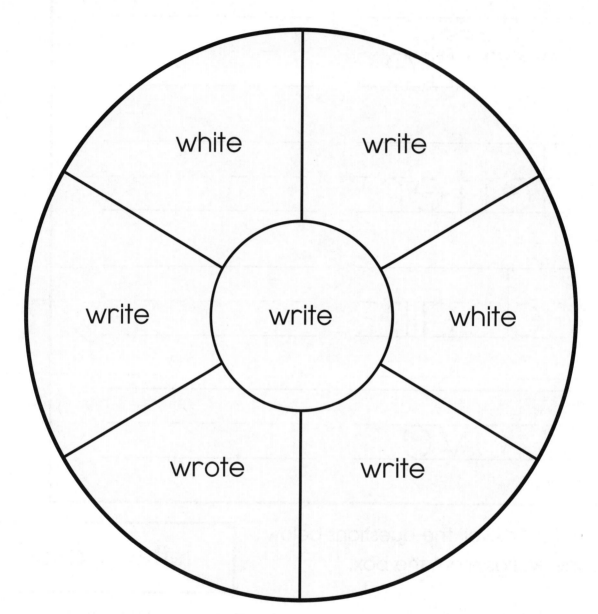

How many did you find? _____

Target words: yesterday, soon, fine

Directions: Write the words below. Say them as you write them.

yesterday

soon

fine

Directions: Circle the word that is the opposite of the underlined word.

1.	I went home <u>yesterday</u>.	house	today	no
2.	The bus will be here <u>soon</u>.	later	sun	hot
3.	We are <u>fine</u>.	sing	song	sick

Now, write this sentence.
I was fine yesterday.

_____

- - - - - - - - - - - - - - - - - -

_____

Target words: write, letter, dear, love, yesterday, soon, fine

Directions: Find and circle the words from the box that are in the letter.

write   letter   dear   love   yesterday   soon   fine

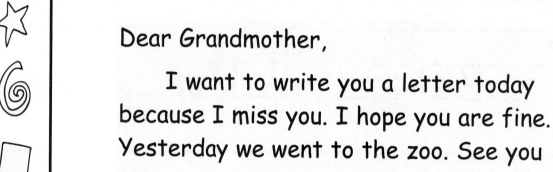

Dear Grandmother,

I want to write you a letter today because I miss you. I hope you are fine. Yesterday we went to the zoo. See you soon.

Love, Sam

Now, write a note to someone. Use the words **dear**, **love**, **soon**, and **fine**.

Target words: cut, grow, longer, keep

Directions: Write the words below. Say them as you write them.

cut

grow

longer

keep

Directions: Find and circle the words from the box.

cut	grow	longer	keep

gone   grow   kite

kite   cat   longer

cat   keep

cut   gone

Target words: want, than, should

Directions: Write the words below. Say them as you write them.

want _ _ _ _ _ _ _ _ _

than _ _ _ _ _ _ _ _ _

should _ _ _ _ _ _ _ _ _

Directions: Color the spaces that have the same word as the one in the middle of the circle.

could | went

want | now

want

went | could

now | want

Now, write a sentence using the word **than** or **should**.

_____

_ _ _ _ _ _ _ _ _ _ _ _ _ _ _

_____

Target words: cut, grow, longer, keep, want, than, should

Directions: Read the story. Find and circle the words from the box.

longer	keep	want	grow
should	cut	want	

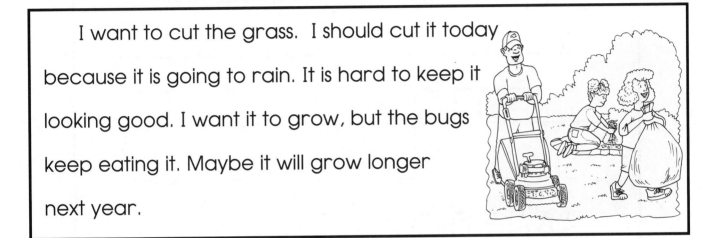

I want to cut the grass. I should cut it today because it is going to rain. It is hard to keep it looking good. I want it to grow, but the bugs keep eating it. Maybe it will grow longer next year.

Directions: Write the letters that are missing in the words below. Use the words from the box to help you.

c _____ t   g _____ ow   t _____ a _____

_____ ee _____   sh _____ _____ l _____   lo _____ _____ e _____

w _____ nt

Target words: these, thing, while

Directions: Write the words below. Say them as you write them.

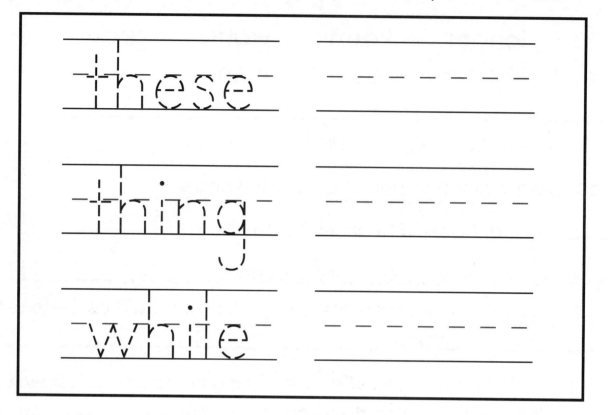

Directions: The words **these** and **thing** are hidden in the lines below. Find and circle them.

t	h	e	s	t	h	e	s	e	t	h	e	s	t	h	e

t	h	i	n	t	h	n	g	t	h	i	n	g	t	h	n

How many did you circle of each?

these _____   **thing** _____

Target words: **which, set**

Directions: Write the words below. Say them as you write them.

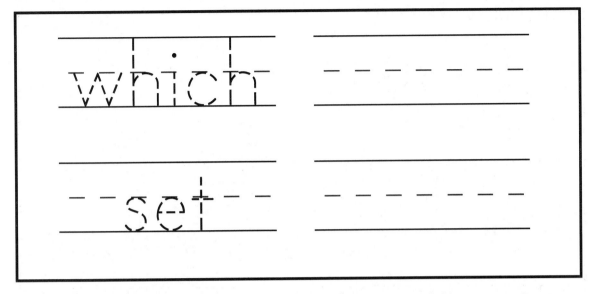

Directions: Color the spaces that have the same word as the one in the middle of the circle.

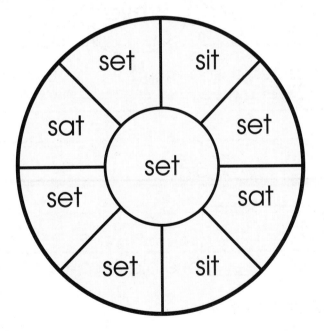

How many spaces did you color? _____

Target words: **these, thing, while, which, set**

Directions: Put the correct words on the footprints to complete the sentences below.

This _____ is big. _____ animal is

here? _____ are big feet! I will hide

_____ it goes by. I do not want it to

knock over my _____ of blocks.

Target words: **first, second, third**

Directions: Write the words below. Say them as you write them.

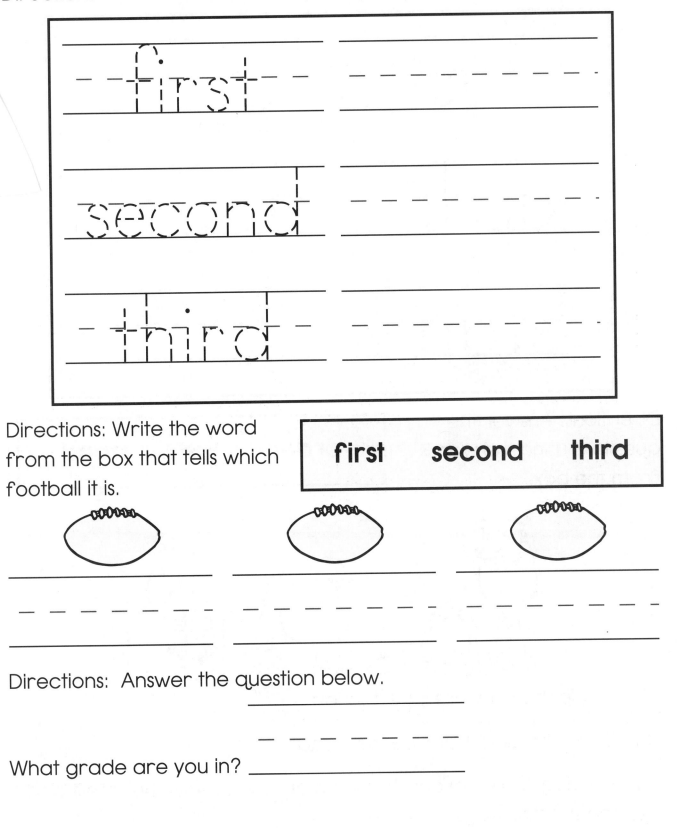

first _____

second _____

third _____

Directions: Write the word from the box that tells which football it is.

first	second	third

_____ _____ _____

Directions: Answer the question below.

_____

What grade are you in? _____

Target words: last, order, stand

Directions: Write the words below. Say them as you write them.

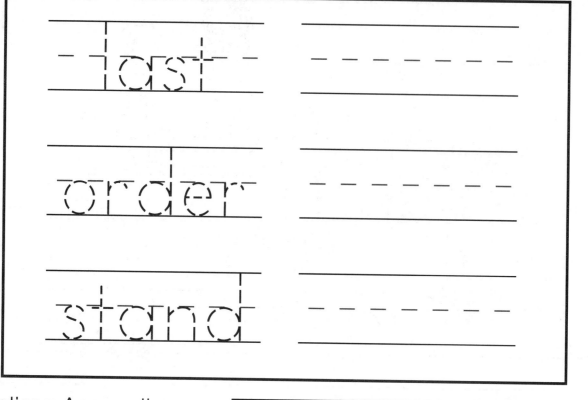

Directions: Answer the questions using the words from the box.

order	last	stand

1. Circle the dog that is next to last.

2. Color the dog that is on the stand.

3. The dogs are in order. Draw an arrow to show the tallest and the shortest dogs.

Target words: **first, second, third, last, order, stan**

Directions: Read the sentences to answer the questions about the picture.

_____

- - - - - - -

1. Who is in the last row? _____

_____

- - - - - - -

2. Who is in the second row? _____

_____

- - - - - - -

3. Who is in the third row? _____

_____

- - - - - - -

4. Who is in the first row? _____

5. Draw where you will stand in the picture.

Target words: where, does, those

Directions: Write the words below. Say them as you write them.

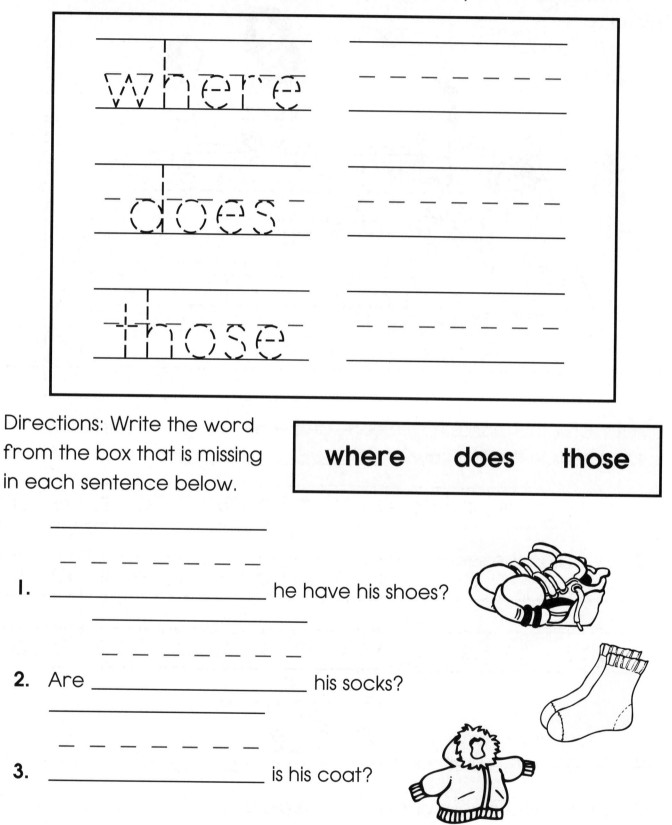

where _____

does _____

those _____

Directions: Write the word from the box that is missing in each sentence below.

where	does	those

1. _____ he have his shoes?

2. Are _____ his socks?

3. _____ is his coat?

Target words: now, seem, shall

Directions: Write the words below. Say them as you write them.

now

seem

shall

Directions: The words **now**, **seem**, and **shall** are hiding in the lines below. Find and circle them. Now, color the boxes.

| n | w | o | n | o | w | o | w | n | o | w | n | o | n | o | w |

| e | m | e | e | m | s | e | e | m | e | e | s | e | e | m | e |

| s | h | l | l | s | h | a | l | l | s | h | a | l | s | h | a |

Directions: What time is it now?

_____

- - - - - - - - - - - - - - - - - - - -

Target words: where, does, those, now, seem, shall

Directions: Write the sentences below.

1. Where are the birds?

- -

_____

2. Does it seem late?

- -

_____

3. No, it doesn't seem late.

- -

_____

4. What time is it now?

- -

_____

5. Who has those shoes?

- -

_____

6. Shall I open the door?

- -

_____

Target words: eyes, ear, hear

Directions: Write the words below. Say them as you write them.

eyes

ear

hear

Directions: Write the word that is missing in each sentence below.

| eyes | ear | hear |

1. I see with my _____.

eyes

ear

2. My _____ can help me _____.

Now, draw a picture of your face. Show where your eyes and ears are. Put a label on them.

Target words: **face, hand, head**

Directions: Write the words below. Say them as you write them.

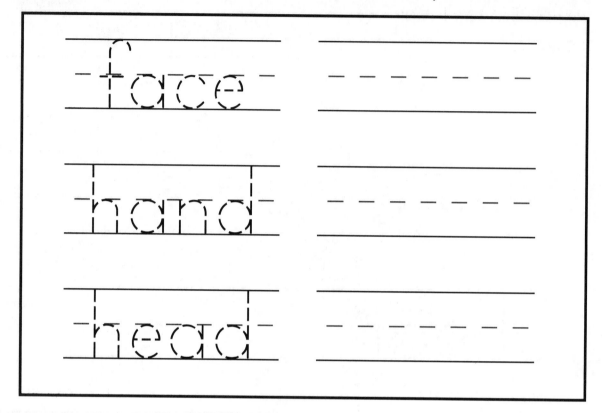

Directions: Fill in the letters that are missing in the words below.

1. h _____ n _____

2. f _____ c _____

3. h _____ _____ d

face → head →
hand →

Now, draw a picture of yourself . Show where your face, hands, and head are. Put labels on your drawing.

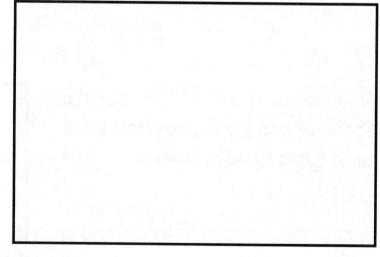

NAME _____

Target words: eyes, ear, hear, face, hand, head

Directions: Use the words from the box to fill in the labels on the drawing.

```
eyes    ear    face
    hand    head
```

_____

_ _ _ _ _ _ _ _ _ _

_____

_____

_ _ _ _ _ _ _ _ _ _

_____

_____

_ _ _ _ _ _ _ _ _ _

_____

_____

_ _ _ _ _ _ _ _ _ _

_____

Now, write this sentence.

I can hear a train.

_____

_ _ _ _ _ _ _ _ _ _

_____

Target words: **fire, sure, start**

Directions: Write the words below. Say them as you write them.

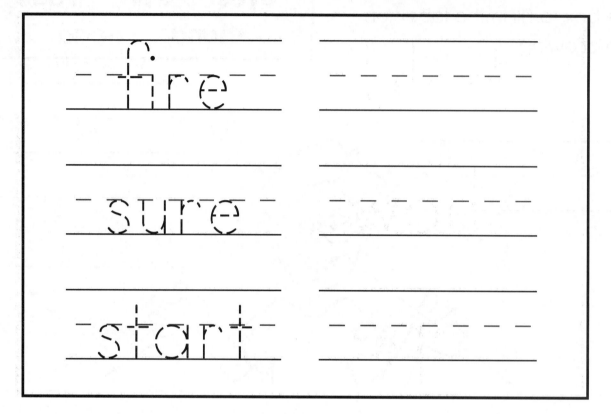

Directions: Color the spaces that have the same word as the one in the middle of the circle.

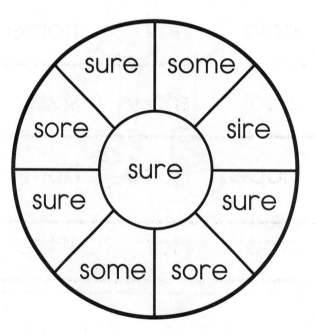

Target words: hold, show, hope, start

Directions: Write the words below. Say them as you write them.

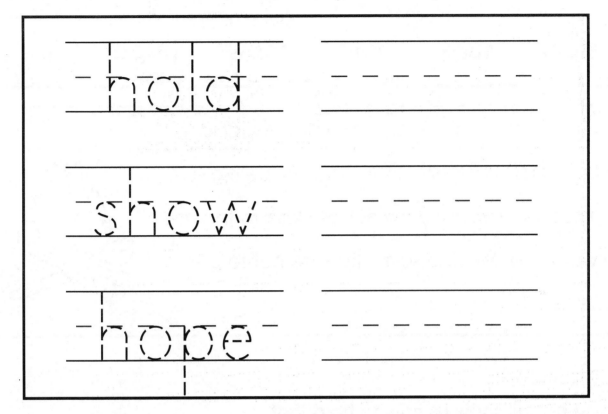

Directions: Circle the three words in each row that are the same.

hope	hold	hold	home	hold
shop	ship	show	show	show
home	hope	hope	ham	hope
start	stop	start	store	start

Target words: fire, sure, start, hold, show, hope

Directions: Read the story. Find and circle the words from the box.

| start | sure | hold | show | hope | fire |

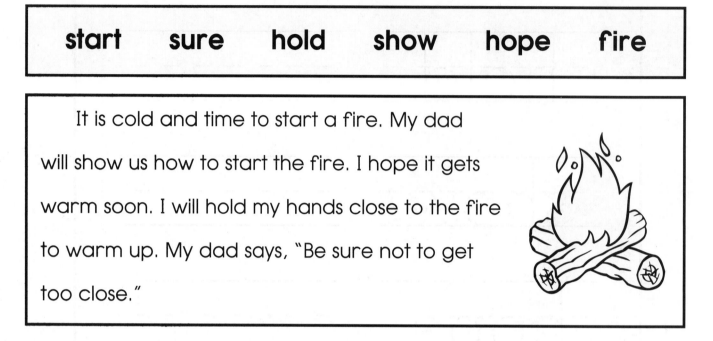

It is cold and time to start a fire. My dad will show us how to start the fire. I hope it gets warm soon. I will hold my hands close to the fire to warm up. My dad says, "Be sure not to get too close."

Now, write this sentence.

I hope he will show us how to hold that.

_____

– –

_____

_____

– –

_____

Target words: right, left, myself

Directions: Write the words below. Say them as you write them.

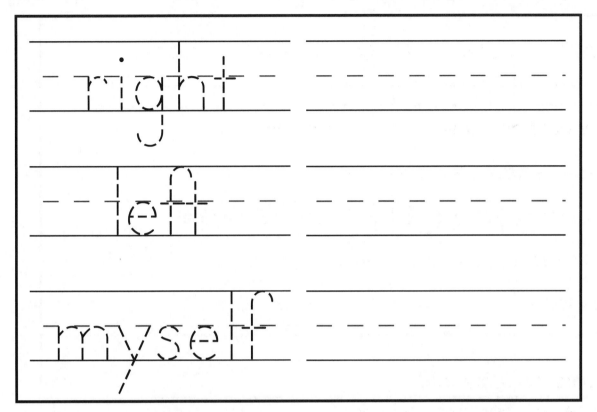

Directions: Read the sentences. Now, follow the directions.

1. Circle the dog on the right.

2. Color the dog on the left.

3. Draw an arrow to the cat on the left.

4. Color the cat on the right.

Now, complete this sentence.

_____

I like myself because _____

_____

_____

Target words: help, small, pair

Directions: Write the words below. Say them as you write them.

Directions: Draw a line to match the pants that have the same words on them.

| help | small | pair |

help   pair   all   small   help   hope   small   pair

Now, write this sentence.

It is a pair of pants.

_____

- - - - - - - - - - - - - -

Target words: **right, left, myself, help, small, pair**

Directions: Find and circle the words from the box. Words can go → or ↓.

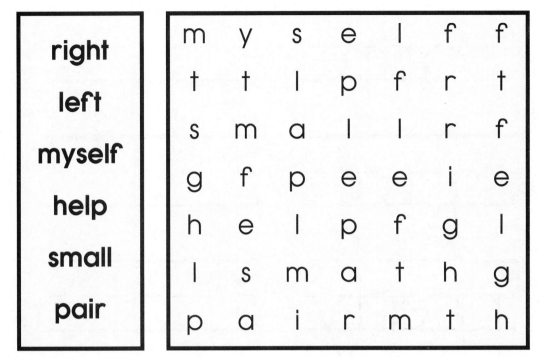

| right | left | myself | help | small | pair |

m	y	s	e	l	f	f
t	t	l	p	f	r	t
s	m	a	l	l	r	f
g	f	p	e	e	i	e
h	e	l	p	f	g	l
l	s	m	a	t	h	g
p	a	i	r	m	t	h

Directions: Draw a line to connect words that are opposites.

yourself	hurt
right	pair
big	left
one	small
help	myself

Now, draw a picture of one of the opposite pairs.

Target words: came, gave, pretty

Directions: Write the words below. Say them as you write them.

came _____   _____

gave _____   _____

pretty _____   _____

Directions: Write these sentences.

My friend came to my party.

_____

_____

Mother gave me a dress.

_____

_____

I had a pretty cake.

_____

_____

Target words: **present, bring, sing**

Directions: Write the words below. Say them as you write them.

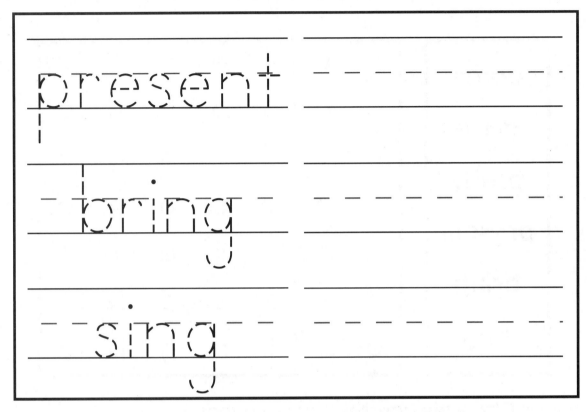

Directions: Color the boxes that have **present**, **bring**, and **sing** in them. Use a different color for each word.

song	present	bang	sing
pretty	bring	song	present
sing	present	bright	sang
present	pretty	sing	bring

How many did you find?

present _____   bring _____   sing _____

Target words: came, gave, pretty, present, bring, sing

Directions: Find and circle the words from the box. Words can go → or ↓.

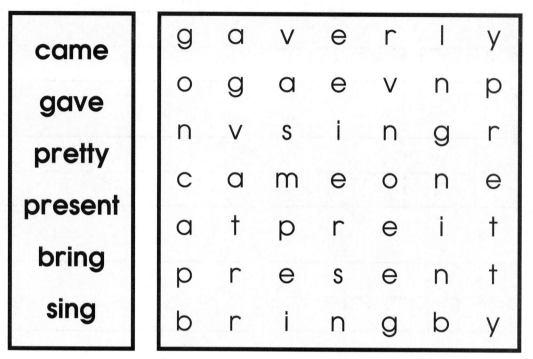

came
gave
pretty
present
bring
sing

g	a	v	e	r	l	y
o	g	a	e	v	n	p
n	v	s	i	n	g	r
c	a	m	e	o	n	e
a	t	p	r	e	i	t
p	r	e	s	e	n	t
b	r	i	n	g	b	y

Directions: Circle the candles that have the words from the box on them.

sing

came

song

come

pretty

present

gift

bring

give

gave

How many candles did you circle? _____

Target words: happy, wish, thank

Directions: Write the words below. Say them as you write them.

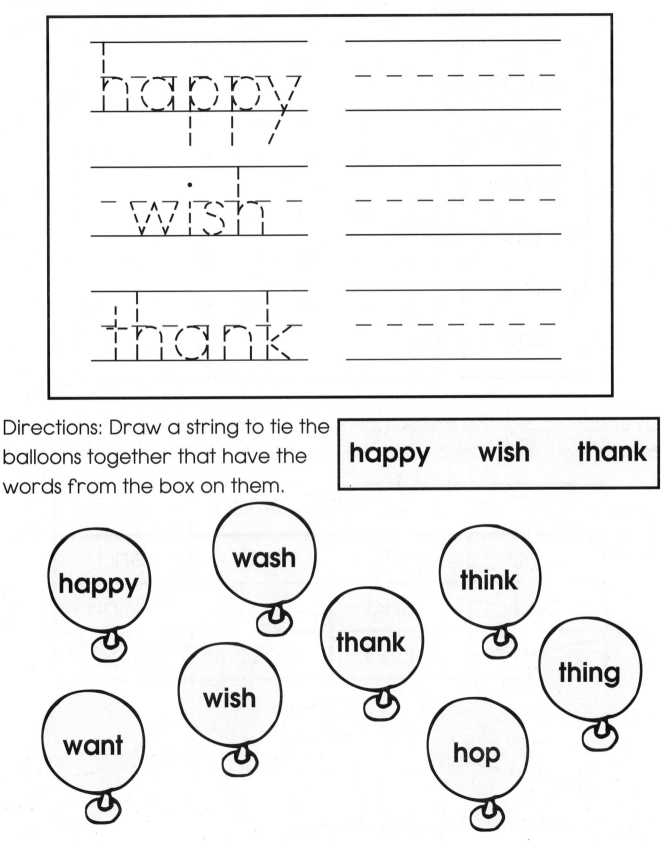

Directions: Draw a string to tie the balloons together that have the words from the box on them.

| happy | wish | thank |

Target words: didn't, end, best

Directions: Write the words below. Say them as you write them.

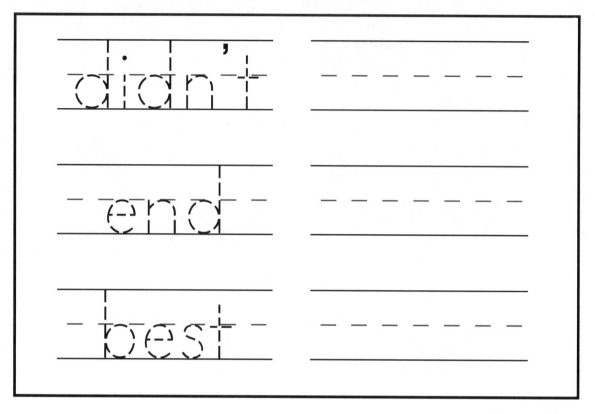

Directions: Color the boxes that have the words **didn't**, **end**, and **best** in them. Use a different color for each word.

don't	end	send	best
send	best	bet	end
end	bend	rest	didn't
best	didn't	did	send

How many did you find?

didn't _____   end _____   best _____

Target words: came, gave, pretty, present, bring,
sing, happy, wish, thank, didn't, end, best

Directions: Read the story. Now, find and circle the words that are
in the box.

| came | gave | pretty | present | bring | sing |
| happy | wish | thank | didn't | end | best |

It was my birthday. Lots of people came to bring me a

present. They also came to sing happy birthday. My mother gave

me a pretty dress. My brother gave me a big book. I have to

thank them all. I wish the day didn't have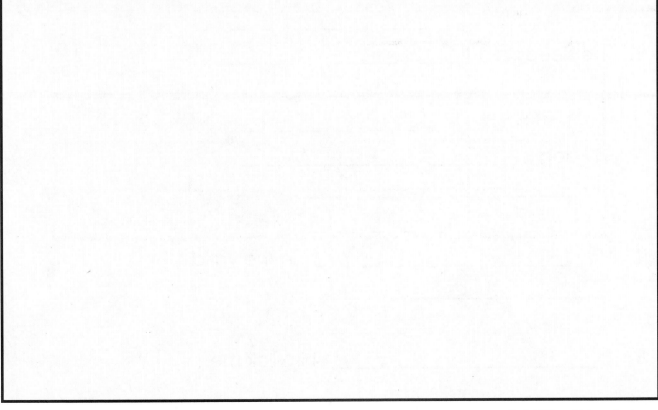

to end. It was the best birthday ever!

Now, draw a picture of your favorite birthday present.

Cloze Sentences

Sight Word Cloze Sentences

Cloze sentences provide young learners an opportunity to use words in context and to gain a better understanding of sentence sense. Use the cloze sentences on the following pages for children to practice selecting the correct word from the word boxes to complete each sentence.

To extend the activity, have children create their own sentences with a missing word. The sentences can also be copied on a separate sheet of paper, cut apart, and reconstructed for sentence sense practice.

Directions: Write the missing word in each sentence.

big   box   got   ran   let

1. I _____ a dog.

2. He sleeps in a _____.

3. My dog is _____.

4. He _____ in the yard.

5. I _____ him lick me.

Cloze Sentences

Directions: Write the missing word in each sentence.

| girl | look | find | sit | run | yes |

1. The _____ had a dog.

2. The dog liked to _____ away fast.

3. The girl had to _____ the dog.

4. She had to _____ for him.

5. Did she find him? _____, she did!

6. Now the girl wants the dog to _____.

Cloze Sentences

Directions: Write the missing word in each sentence.

sleep	bed	morning	school	early	night

1. It is dark at _____.

2. I get in my _____.

3. I have to go to _____ now.

4. In the _____ I get up.

5. I have to get up _____.

6. And I have to go to _____.

Cloze Sentences

Directions: Write the missing word in each sentence.

open close leave door don't off

1. I see a _____ .

2. It is _____ .

3. Don't _____ the door.

4. _____ the light on.

5. Please don't turn _____ the light.

6. I _____ like the dark.

Cloze Sentences

Directions: Write the missing word in each sentence.

car	far	ride	took	around	back

1. We went for a _____.

2. We drove in the _____.

3. The ride _____ a long time.

4. We went _____ away.

5. Then we went _____ the park.

6. At last we came _____ home.

Cloze Sentences

Directions: Write the missing word in each sentence.

done	wash	clean	water	carry	warm

1. I have to _____ the dishes.

2. I will _____ them to the sink.

3. I need to get some _____.

4. The water is not too _____.

5. Now the dishes are _____.

6. Now I am _____!

Cloze Sentences

Directions: Write the missing word in each sentence.

| coat | cold | dress | kind | better | clothes |

1. It is _____ outside.

2. I _____ not go outside yet.

3. My _____ is not very warm.

4. First, I need to put on some warm _____.

5. My mom gives me a warm _____.

6. She is very _____ to me.

Cloze Sentences

Directions: Write the missing word in each sentence.

more	always	ate	food	full	most

1. The _____ is good here.

2. I _____ eat too much.

3. My dad eats the _____ food.

4. He _____ all the food on his plate!

5. Now he is _____.

6. He can not eat any _____.

Cloze Sentences

Directions: Write the missing word in each sentence.

| dear | letter | soon | love | fine | yesterday |

1. Bob wrote a _____ to his sister.

2. He wrote, "_____ Pat, how are you?"

3. "I am _____," Bob wrote.

4. _____ I went to the park."

5. He signed it, "_____, Bob."

6. He will mail it _____.

Cloze Sentences

Directions: Write the missing word in each sentence.

ear	hand	head	eyes	hear	face

1. I can _____ the dog bark.

2. I can hear with my _____.

3. I have two _____.

4. I can see my _____ in the mirror.

5. My hat is on my _____.

6. A _____ has five fingers.

Scrambled Sentences

Sight Word Scrambled Sentences

Once children can recognize and understand individual sight words in print, they are ready to use them to build sentences. This is the exciting next step in the reading process and, for many children, the moment when they say, "I'm really reading!"

The following scrambled sentences build upon sight word knowledge and are designed to help children learn—and demonstrate—sentence sense by putting individual words into the correct order so each sentence makes sense. The sight words used in these sentences follow the order in which they have been introduced.

The sentences can be used in a number of ways, depending on each child's developmental level. First, encourage the child to look for helpful sentence-sense clues, such as a capitalized word that would indicate the beginning of the sentence and a word with punctuation that would indicate the end of the sentence. Then, have the child say all the words aloud, starting with the capitalized word and ending with the punctuated word. Ask the child if what he or she said aloud makes sense, and, if necessary, encourage him or her to rearrange the "middle" words around while saying them aloud until they are in the correct order. Then, have the child write the unscrambled sentence on the line provided. You may want to encourage the child to write the sentence's sight words in different-colored crayons or markers, or to use the sight word flash cards to find the matching words used in the sentence.

You may also want to have the child write the unscrambled sentence on a separate sheet of paper and cut it apart into individual words. Then, using the child's hand-written unscrambled sentence in the workbook as a model, have him or her reassemble the cut-apart words into the sentence. This activity works well as a self-checking review. Or have the child distribute the cut-apart words to other children, who can then reassemble them in the correct order. An activity of this type can also be used with sentences that the children dictate or write themselves on a separate sheet of paper. Extending this activity to sentences that children compose themselves increases their level of engagement and provides an opportunity for individualizing their learning.

Scrambled Sentences

say   I   May   this?

_____

- - - - - - - - - - - - - - - - - -

_____

likes   He   fast.   run   to

_____

- - - - - - - - - - - - - - - - - -

_____

him.   had   to   She   for   look

_____

- - - - - - - - - - - - - - - - - -

_____

buy   she   Can   pencil?   a

_____

- - - - - - - - - - - - - - - - - -

_____

Scrambled Sentences

under   tree.   rock   a   A   is

_____

- -

_____

will   the   car.   I   leave

_____

- -

_____

door.   Please   the   close

_____

- -

_____

get   Let's   pumpkin.   another

_____

- -

_____

- -

_____

Scrambled Sentences

fast.   That   plane   can   fly

_____

- -

_____

dad   most.   the   eats   My

_____

- -

_____

five   hand   has   fingers.   A

_____

- -

_____

letter   will   write   a   I   you.   to

_____

- -

_____

- -

Scrambled Sentences

a He run. hit home

_____

- - - - - - - - - - - - - - - - - -

_____

soon write letter. I will a

_____

- - - - - - - - - - - - - - - - - -

_____

can I see eyes. with my

_____

- - - - - - - - - - - - - - - - - -

_____

goes here. It right

_____

- - - - - - - - - - - - - - - - - -

_____

Sight Word Flash Cards

On the following pages are flash cards for all of the sight words used in this book. For ease of use, they are presented in the order of introduction in the book. Laminating the cards would also help make them durable. Punching a hole in each card and keeping them on a ring for each child is also a good way to keep the cards organized and easy to use.

There are many ways to use these cards. Listed below are some games and activities to help children learn to recognize the sight words:

- Sort the cards by sight words with the same beginning letter

- Find sight words that rhyme, and write other words that rhyme with the sight words on a dry erase board or separate sheet of paper.

- Sort the cards to make pairs of sight words that begin with the same letter. Play the "Memory" game using these words—players don't get to keep the pair unless they can read both words. As an extension of this, also have players use the words in sentences.

- Use a timer to see how quickly each sight word is recognized. Begin with a small number of cards. Add more cards once increased speed and confidence is achieved.

- Put the sight words in alphabetical order.

- Come up with another word that begins with the same sound as each sight word.

am	big
box	ran
let	got
play	ball

hat	call
jump	sat
red	black
yellow	green

white	blue
brown	color
say	ask
friend	way

may	today
girl	look
find	dog
run	sit

yes	four
five	six
seven	eight
nine	ten

money	buy
under	upon
next	near
high	tree

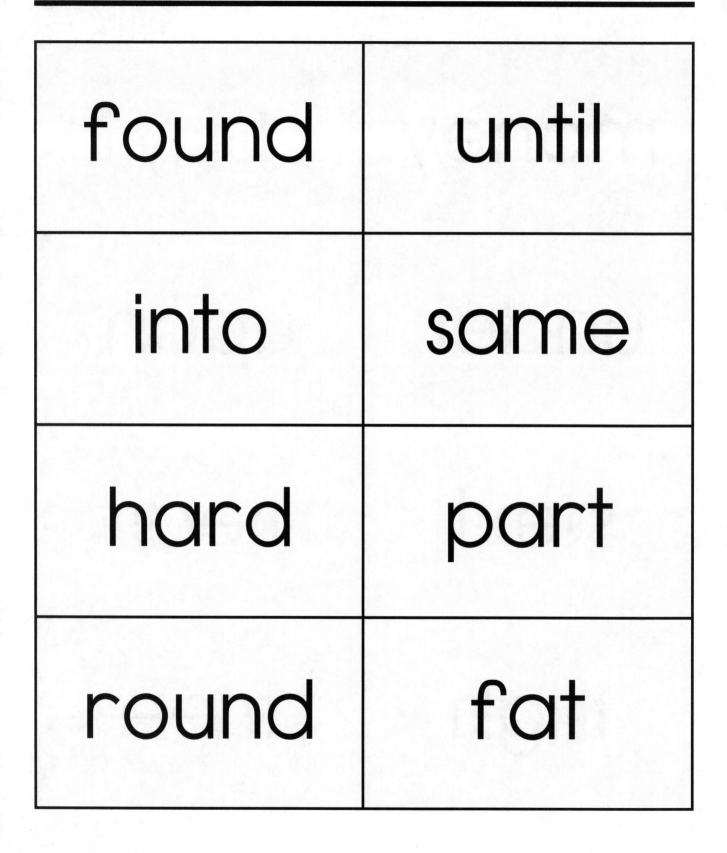

found	until
into	same
hard	part
round	fat

funny	might
saw	only
such	never
live	house

home	mother
sister	brother
each	own
name	year

also	fall
sleep	morning
night	bed
o'clock	early

school	open
close	leave
off	door
don't	read

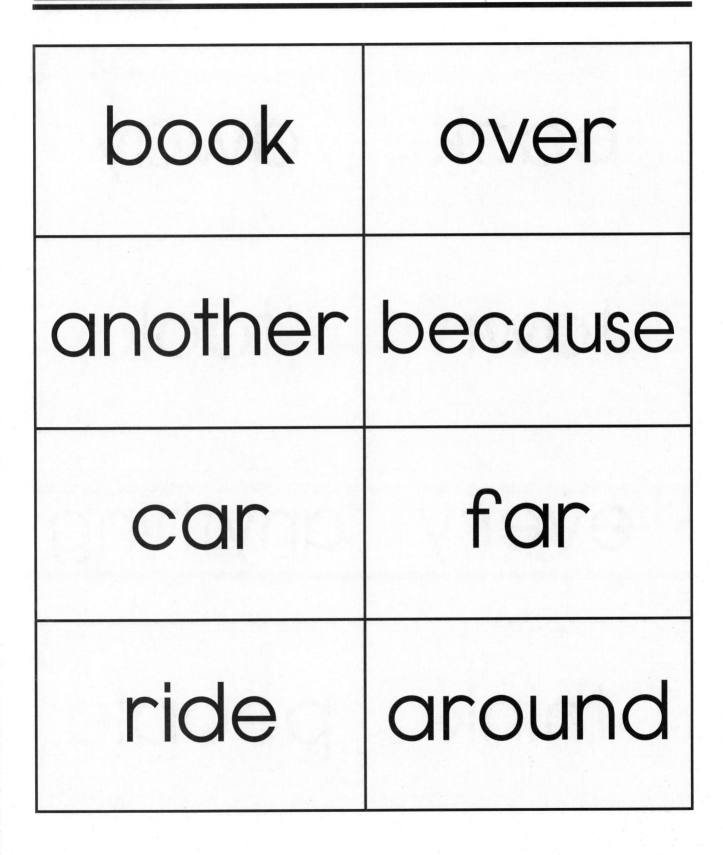

book	over
another	because
car	far
ride	around

back	away
town	took
every	anything
think	people

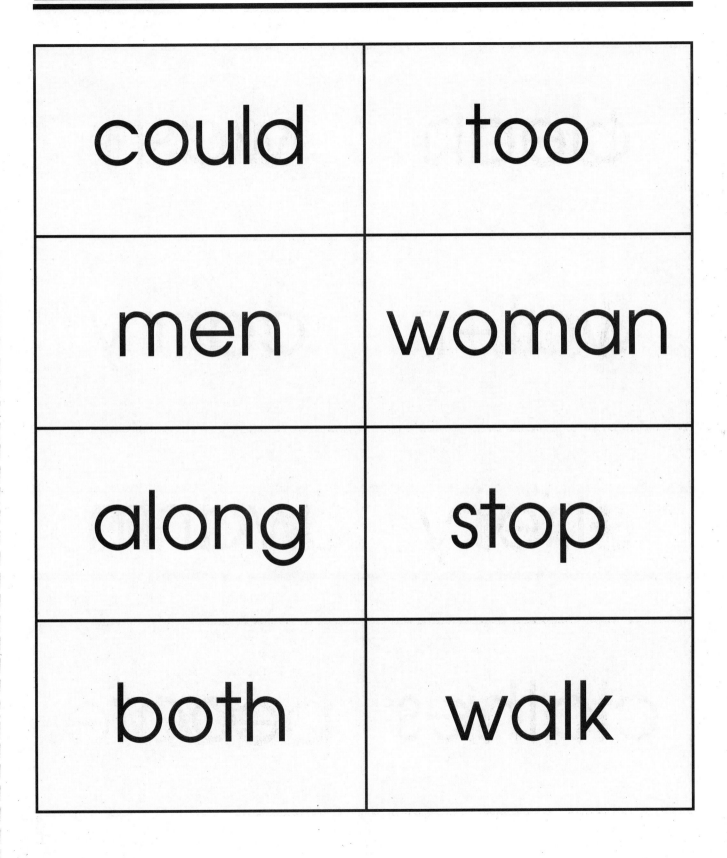

could	too
men	woman
along	stop
both	walk

clean	wash
water	carry
hot	warm
clothes	coat

cold	kind
dress	better
please	tell
once	use

made	fly
fast	goes
try	though
why	food

ate	full
most	more
always	write
letter	dear

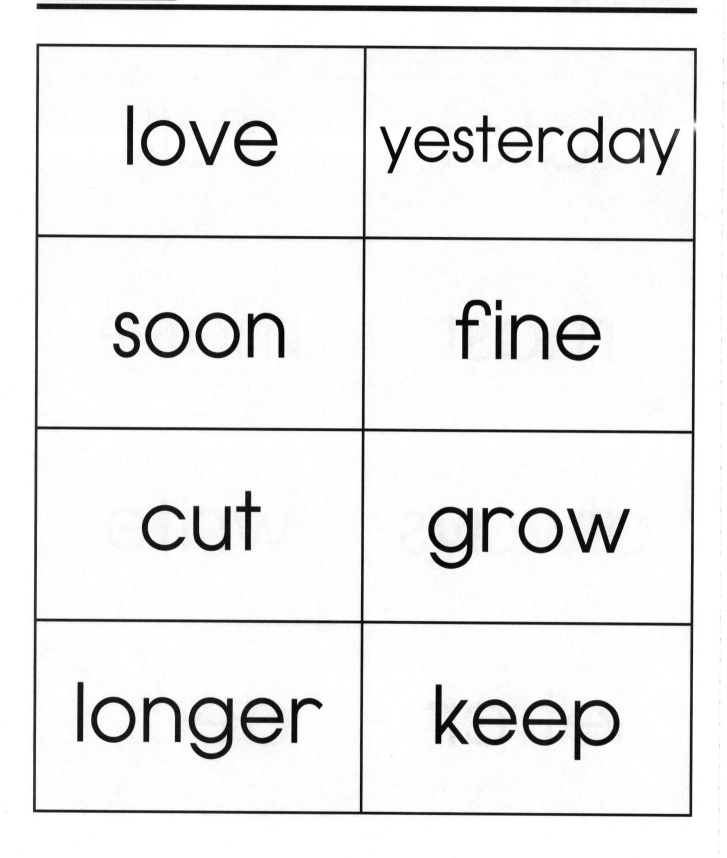

love	yesterday
soon	fine
cut	grow
longer	keep

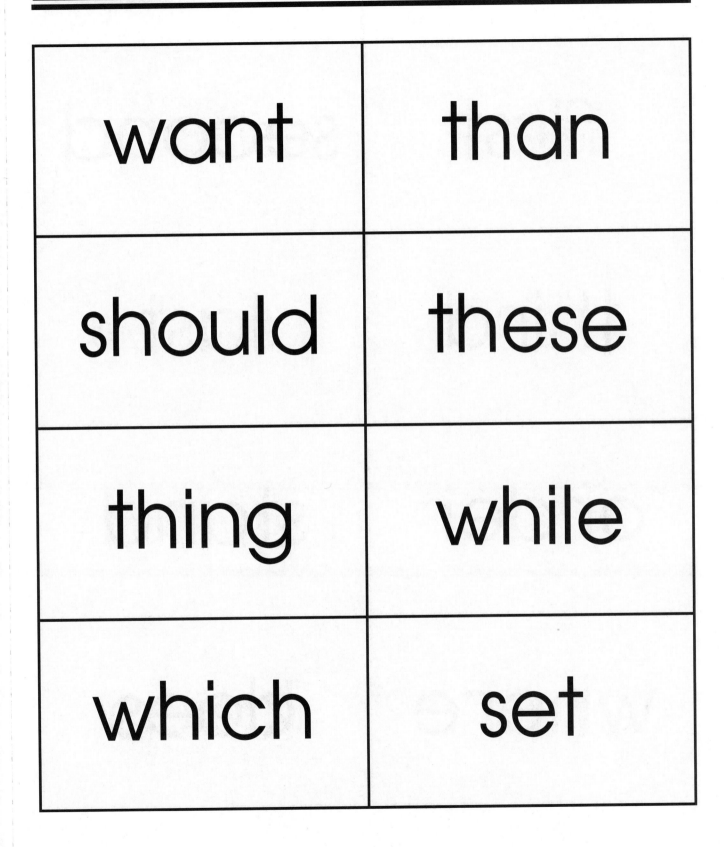

want	than
should	these
thing	while
which	set

first	second
third	last
order	stand
where	does

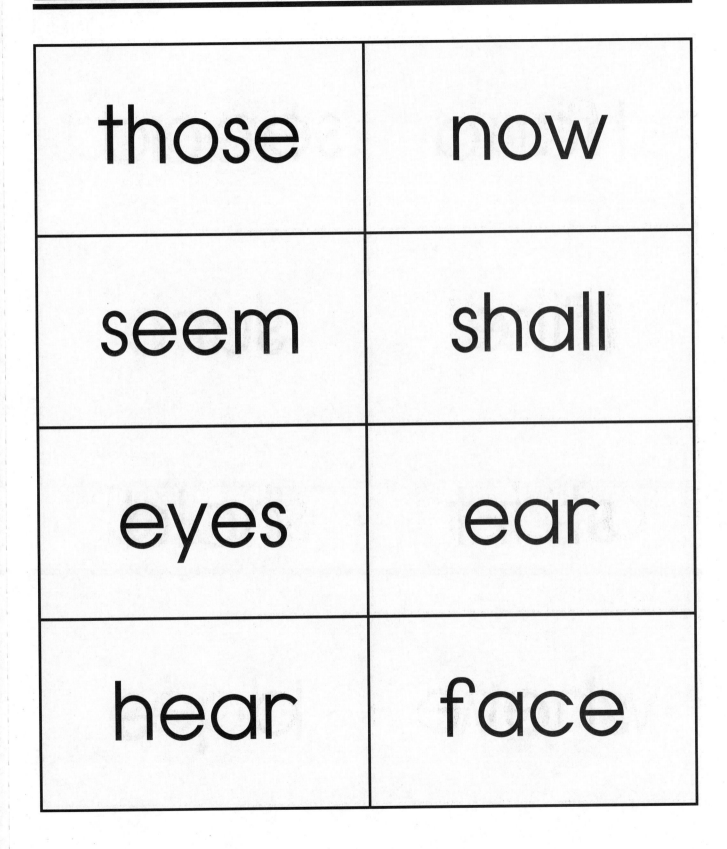

those	now
seem	shall
eyes	ear
hear	face

hand	head
fire	sure
start	hold
show	hope

right	left
myself	help
small	pair
come	gave

pretty	present
bring	sing
happy	wish
thank	didn't

end	best

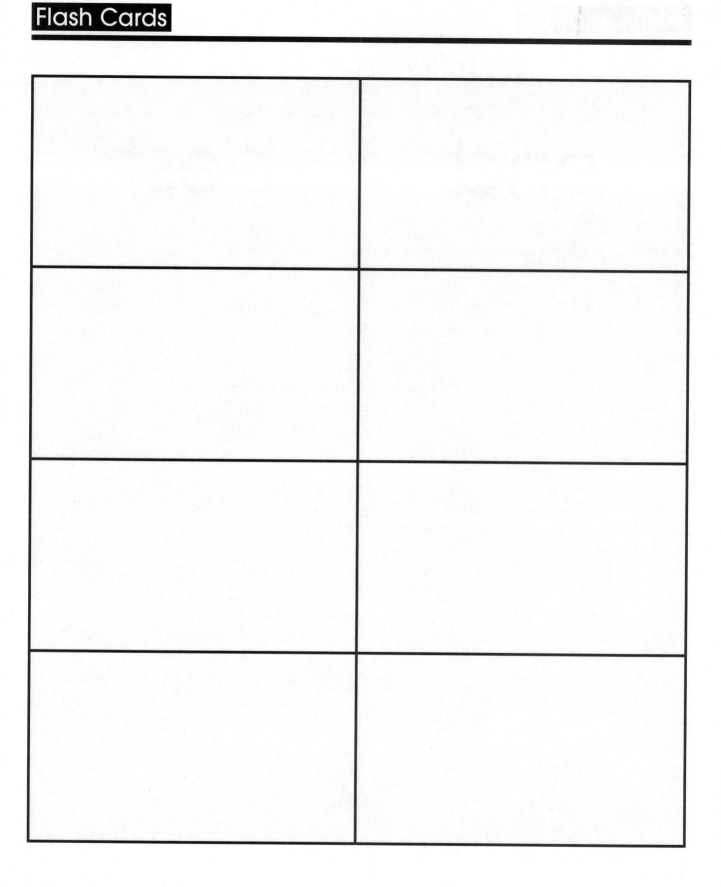

Fry Instant Sight Word List

First One Hundred Words

a	can	her	many	see	us
about	come	here	me	she	very
after	day	him	much	so	was
again	did	his	my	some	we
all	do	how	new	take	were
an	down	I	no	that	what
and	eat	if	not	the	when
any	for	in	of	their	which
are	from	is	old	them	who
as	get	it	on	then	will
at	give	just	one	there	with
be	go	know	or	they	work
been	good	like	other	this	would
before	had	little	our	three	you
boy	has	long	out	to	your
but	have	make	put	two	
by	he	man	said	up	

Fry Instant Sight Word List

Second One Hundred Words

also	color	home	must	red	think
am	could	house	name	right	too
another	dear	into	near	run	tree
away	each	kind	never	saw	under
back	ear	last	next	say	until
ball	end	leave	night	school	upon
because	far	left	only	seem	use
best	find	let	open	shall	want
better	first	live	over	should	way
big	five	look	own	soon	where
black	found	made	people	stand	while
book	four	may	play	such	white
both	friend	men	please	sure	wish
box	girl	more	present	tell	why
bring	got	morning	pretty	than	year
call	hand	most	ran	these	
came	high	mother	read	thing	

Fry Instant Sight Word List

Third One Hundred Words

along	didn't	food	keep	sat	though
always	does	full	letter	second	today
anything	dog	funny	longer	set	took
around	don't	gave	love	seven	town
ask	door	goes	might	show	try
ate	dress	green	money	sing	turn
bed	early	grow	myself	sister	walk
brown	eight	hat	now	sit	warm
buy	every	happy	o'clock	six	wash
car	eyes	hard	off	sleep	water
carry	face	head	once	small	woman
clean	fall	hear	order	start	write
close	fast	help	pair	stop	yellow
clothes	fat	hold	part	ten	yes
coat	fine	hope	ride	thank	yesterday
cold	fire	hot	round	third	
cut	fly	jump	same	those	

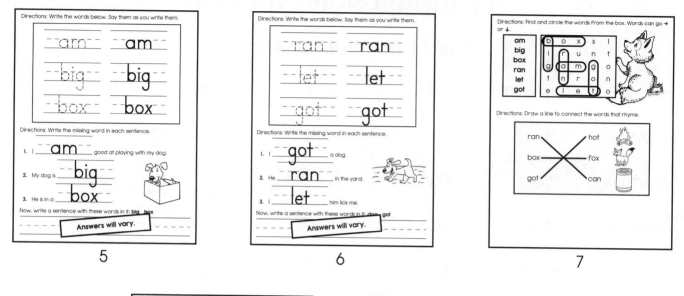

Directions: Write the words below. Say them as you write them.

am	am
big	big
box	box

Directions: Write the missing word in each sentence.

1. I __am__ good at playing with my dog.
2. My dog is __big__
3. He is in a __box__

Now, write a sentence with these words in it: **big box**

Answers will vary.

5

Directions: Write the words below. Say them as you write them.

ran	ran
let	let
got	got

Directions: Write the missing word in each sentence.

1. I __got__ a dog.
2. He __ran__ in the yard.
3. I __let__ him lick me.

Now, write a sentence with these words in it: **dog got**

Answers will vary.

6

Directions: Find and circle the words from the box. Words can go → or ↓.

am big box ran let got

Directions: Draw a line to connect the words that rhyme.

ran — hot
box — fox
got — can

7

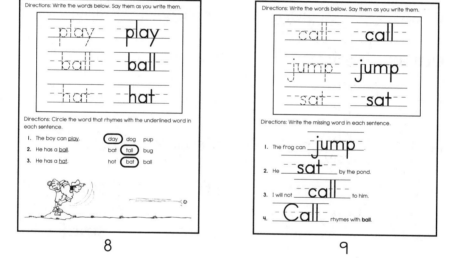

Directions: Write the words below. Say them as you write them.

play	play
ball	ball
hat	hat

Directions: Circle the word that rhymes with the underlined word in each sentence.

1. The boy can play.   (day) dog pup
2. He has a ball.   bat (tall) bug
3. He has a hat.   hot (bat) ball

8

Directions: Write the words below. Say them as you write them.

call	call
jump	jump
sat	sat

Directions: Write the missing word in each sentence.

1. The frog can __jump__
2. He __sat__ by the pond.
3. I will not __call__ to him.
4. __Call__ rhymes with **ball**.

9

Directions: Circle each set of footballs that have rhyming words on them.

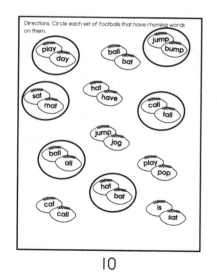

play / day
ball / bat
jump / bump
sat / mat
hat / have
call / tall
jump / jog
ball / all
play / pop
hat / bat
cat / call
is / sat

10

Directions: Write the words below. Say them as you write them.

red	red
black	black
yellow	yellow
green	green

Directions: Write the missing word in each sentence.

1. A bear is __black__
2. An apple is __red/yellow/green__

11

Directions: Write the words below. Say them as you write them.

white	white
blue	blue
brown	brown
color	color

Directions: Write the missing word in each sentence.

| white | blue | brown | color |

1. I can color the bear __brown__
2. The snowman is __white__

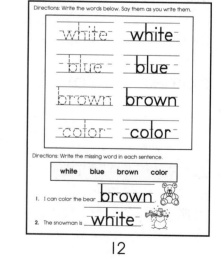

12

Directions:
1. Color bear number 1 blue.
2. Color bear number 2 green.
3. Color bear number 3 brown.
4. Color bear number 4 yellow.
5. Color bear number 5 white.
6. Color bear number 6 black.
7. Color bear number 7 red.

blue — 1
green — 2
brown — 3
yellow — 4
white — 5
black — 6
red — 7

13

Directions: Write the words below. Say them as you write them.

say   say
ask   ask
friend   friend

Directions: The words **say, ask,** and **friend** are hiding in the lines below. Find and circle them. Now, color the boxes.

a s a y a s a y s a a s a y s y
s a k s a s k a s s a s k a s k
r e i n d r f r i e n d f r e n d

Hi, how are you?   I'm fine. How are you?

14

Directions: Write the words below. Say them as you write them.

way   way
may   may
today   today

Directions: Write the missing word in each sentence. Now, circle the words in each sentence that rhyme.

1. This is the (way) I want to (play).
2. (May) (say) this?
3. (today) (Monday).

Directions: Write 3 more words that rhyme with way and may.

Answers will vary.

15

Directions: The letters in the words are mixed up. Unscramble them to write each word correctly. Use the words from the box to help you.

| today | way | ask | say | friend |

1. (ksa) ask
2. (yas) say
3. (drfeni) friend
4. (doayt) today
5. (wya) way

Directions: Unscramble the words in this sentence. Now, write the sentence.
I play with my drfeni.

I play with my friend.

16

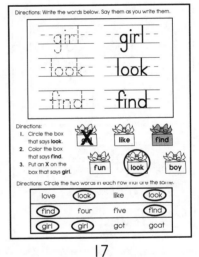

Directions: Write the words below. Say them as you write them.

girl   girl
look   look
find   find

Directions:
1. Circle the box that says **look**.
2. Color the box that says **find**.
3. Put an **X** on the box that says **girl**.

girl   like   find
fun   look   boy

Directions: Circle the two words in each row that are the same.

love	(look)	like	(look)
(find)	four	five	(find)
(girl)	(girl)	got	goat

17

Directions: Write the words below. Say them as you write them.

dog   dog
run   run
sit   sit
yes   yes

Directions: Find and circle the dog bones with the words from the box on them.

| dog | run | sit | yes |

(yes)   (ran)   (dog)   yet
set   (run)   day   (sit)

How many did you circle? __4__

18

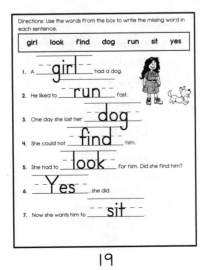

Directions: Use the words from the box to write the missing word in each sentence.

| girl | look | find | dog | run | sit | yes |

1. A __girl__ had a dog.
2. He liked to __run__ fast.
3. One day she lost her __dog__.
4. She could not __find__ him.
5. She had to __look__ for him. Did she find him?
6. __Yes__, she did.
7. Now she wants him to __sit__.

19

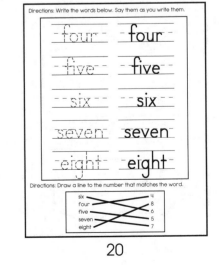

Directions: Write the words below. Say them as you write them.

four   four
five   five
six   six
seven   seven
eight   eight

Directions: Draw a line to the number that matches the word.

six — 8
four — 4
five — 6
seven — 5
eight — 7

20

Directions: Write the words below. Say them as you write them.

nine nine
ten ten
money money
buy buy

Directions: Write the missing word in each sentence. Then, write the answers.

1. Can she __buy__ a pencil?

2. How much __money__ does she have?

21

Directions: Draw a line from each box to the word that tells how many coins there are.

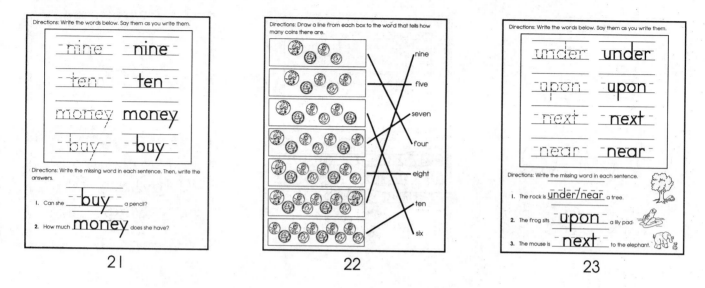

nine
five
seven
four
eight
ten
six

22

Directions: Write the words below. Say them as you write them.

under under
upon upon
next next
near near

Directions: Write the missing word in each sentence.

1. The rock is __under/near__ a tree.

2. The frog sits __upon__ a lily pad.

3. The mouse is __next__ to the elephant.

23

Directions: Write the words below. Say them as you write them.

high high
tree tree
found found

Directions: Unscramble the letters to make the words from the box. Now, write the correct word next to each apple.

ghhi __high__

etre __tree__

dnofu __found__

24

Directions: Write the words below. Say them as you write them.

until until
into into
same same

Directions: Color the apples that have the same words on them.

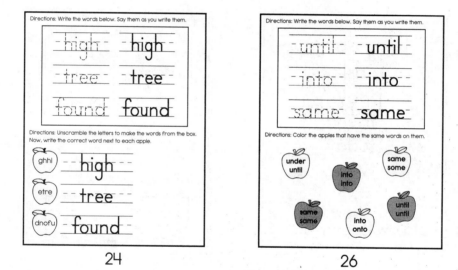

under until

into into

same some

same same

into onto

until until

26

Directions: Write the words below. Say them as you write them.

hard hard
part part
round round

Directions: Draw a line to connect the bouncing balls to get to the basket. Use the words from the box.

round hard part

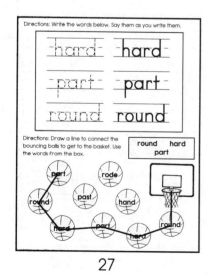

part rode
round past hand
hard part round
hard

27

Directions: Write the missing word in each sentence.

until into same hard round

1. An apple is __round/hard__

2. It is __hard/round__

3. You can bite __into__ it.

4. Eat it all __until__ it is gone.

5. The two parts are the __same__

Directions: Color the spaces that have words that rhyme with the word in the middle.

past farm
art part cart
dart smart

28

Directions: Write the words below. Say them as you write them.

fat fat
funny funny
might might

Directions: Draw a line to connect the words that rhyme.

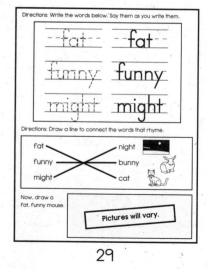

fat night
funny bunny
might cat

Now, draw a fat, funny mouse.

Pictures will vary.

29

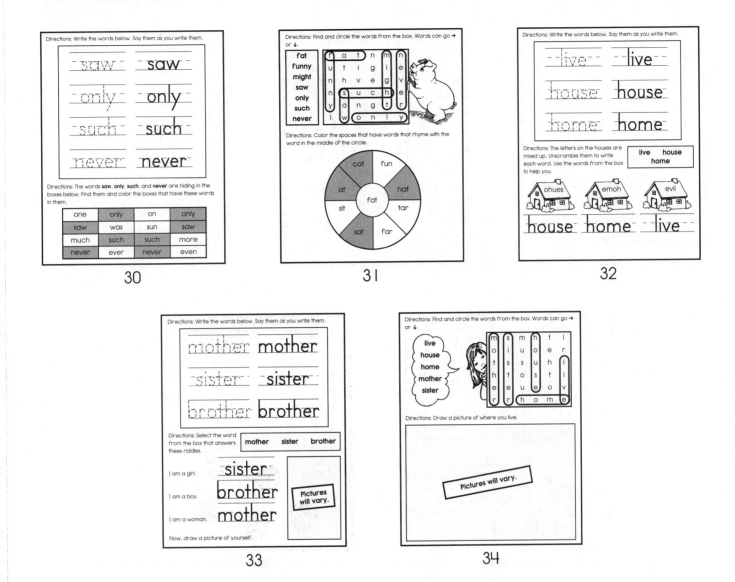

30

31

32

33

34

37

39

40

Answer Key

42

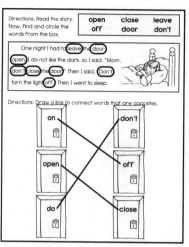

43

Directions: Write the words below. Say them as you write them.

read | - - - -
book | - - - -
over | - - - -

Directions: Several words below are mixed up. Unscramble the letters and write all the words on the lines. Use the words from the box.

| book | over | read | and | can | I | a |

I nac daer a kobo
I can read a book
voer. dna voer.
over and over

44

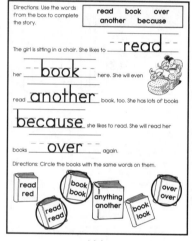

46

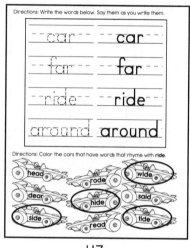

47

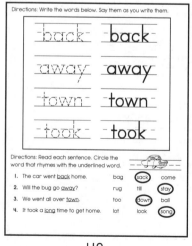

48

49

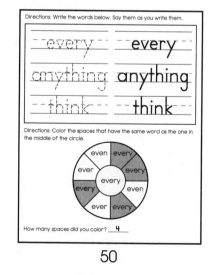

50

Answer Key

Answer Key

Directions: Write the words below. Say them as you write them.

people	people
could	could
too	too

Directions: Unscramble the letters to make the words from the box. Now, write them on the line under each book.

| could | people | too |

oto   eopple   dcluo

too   people   could

Now, write this sentence.
People could read too.

People could read too.

51

Directions: Read the story. Now, find and circle the words from the box.

| every | anything | think | people | could | too |

I love to read (every) book I can.
I tell my friends that they (could) (too)
They (could) read as many books as I do.
(think) lots of (people) (could) read (anything)
they want. Let's read!

Now, write a sentence telling what you think people would like to read about.

Answers will vary.

52

Directions: Write the words below. Say them as you write them.

men	men
woman	woman
along	along

Directions: Color the spaces that have the same word as the one in the middle of the circle.

How many spaces did you color? __5__

53

Directions: Write the words below. Say them as you write them.

stop	stop
both	both
walk	walk

Directions: Look at the picture. Which sentence tells about the picture? Put an **X** by that sentence.

1. _____ Both men are driving a car.
2. _____ Both men will stop eating.
3. __X__ Both men walk by the stop sign.
4. _____ The men both jump.

54

Directions: To get to the street, draw a line to connect the stop signs that contain the words from the box. The first one is done for you.

| men | woman | along | stop | both | walk |

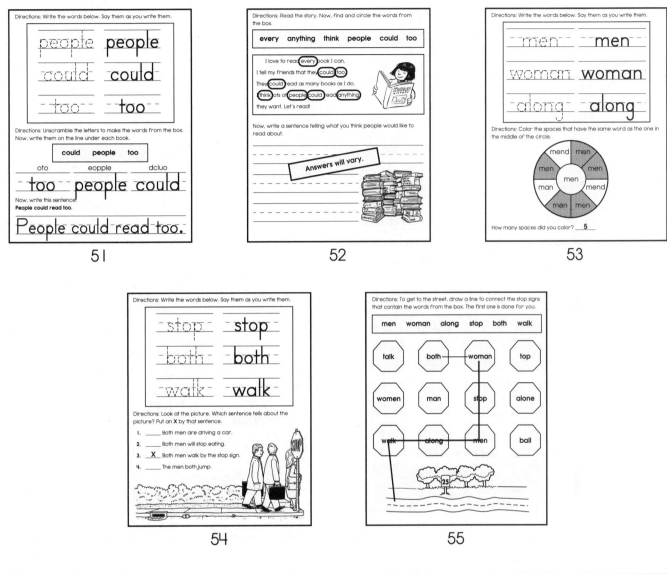

55

Directions: Write the words below. Say them as you write them.

clean	clean
wash	wash
water	water

Directions: Unscramble the words on the wash tubs. Now, write each word on the line. Use the words from the box to help you.

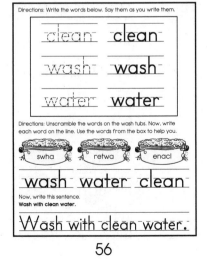

swha   retwa   enacl

wash   water   clean

Now, write this sentence.
Wash with clean water.

Wash with clean water.

56

Directions: Write the words below. Say them as you write them.

carry	cary
hot	hot
warm	warm

Directions: Draw a line from each bucket to its matching word.

57

Directions: Unscramble the words from the box. Write each word on the line under its bubble. Now, write the words on the wash tubs in alphabetical order.

| clean | wash | water | hot | warm |

naelc   hwas

clean   wash

rweat   toh

water   hot

awrm

warm

58

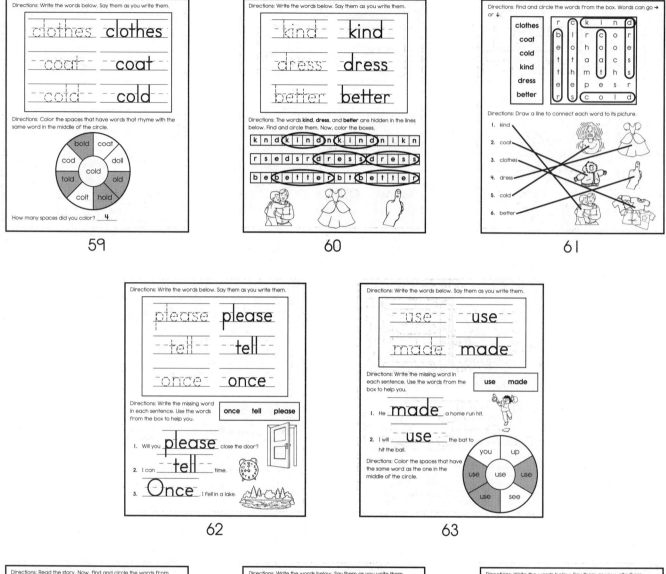

59

Directions: Write the words below. Say them as you write them.

clothes | clothes
coat | coat
cold | cold

Directions: Color the spaces that have words that rhyme with the same word in the middle of the circle.

bold · coat · cod · doll · cold · told · old · colt · hold

How many spaces did you color? __4__

60

Directions: Write the words below. Say them as you write them.

kind | kind
dress | dress
better | better

Directions: The words **kind**, **dress**, and **better** are hidden in the lines below. Find and circle them. Now, color the boxes.

k n d (k i n d) n (k i n d) n i k n
r s e d s r (d r e s s) (d r e s s)
b e (b e t t e r) b t (b e t t e r)

61

Directions: Find and circle the words from the box. Words can go → or ↓.

clothes / coat / cold / kind / dress / better

Directions: Draw a line to connect each word to its picture.

1. kind
2. coat
3. clothes
4. dress
5. cold
6. better

62

Directions: Write the words below. Say them as you write them.

please | please
tell | tell
once | once

Directions: Write the missing word in each sentence. Use the words from the box to help you.

once   tell   please

1. Will you **please** close the door?
2. I can **tell** time.
3. **Once** I fell in a lake.

63

Directions: Write the words below. Say them as you write them.

use | use
made | made

Directions: Write the missing word in each sentence. Use the words from the box to help you.

use   made

1. He **made** a home run hit.
2. I will **use** the bat to hit the ball.

Directions: Color the spaces that have the same word as the one in the middle of the circle.

you · up · use · use · use · use · see

64

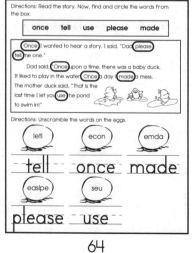

Directions: Read the story. Now, find and circle the words from the box.

once   tell   use   please   made

(Once) I wanted to hear a story. I said, "Dad (please) (tell) me one."

Dad said, (Once) upon a time, there was a baby duck. It liked to play in the water. (Once) a day it (made) a mess. The mother duck said, "That is the last time I let you (use) the pond to swim in!"

Directions: Unscramble the words on the eggs.

letl — **tell**
econ — **once**
emda — **made**
easlpe — **please**
seu — **use**

65

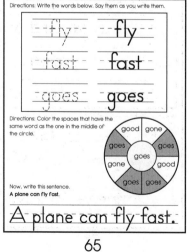

Directions: Write the words below. Say them as you write them.

fly | fly
fast | fast
goes | goes

Directions: Color the spaces that have the same word as the one in the middle of the circle.

good · gone · goes · goes · gone · goes · good · goes · goes

Now, write this sentence.
A plane can fly fast.

A plane can fly fast.

66

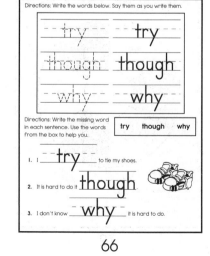

Directions: Write the words below. Say them as you write them.

try | try
though | though
why | why

Directions: Write the missing word in each sentence. Use the words from the box to help you.

try   though   why

1. I **try** to tie my shoes.
2. It is hard to do it, **though**.
3. I don't know **why** it is hard to do.

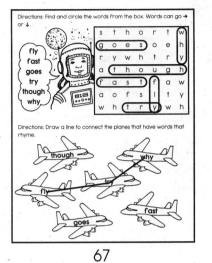

Directions: Find and circle the words from the box. Words can go → or ↓.

Directions: Draw a line to connect the planes that have words that rhyme.

67

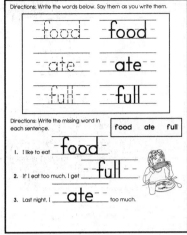

Directions: Write the words below. Say them as you write them.

Directions: Write the missing word in each sentence.

| food | ate | full |

1. I like to eat __food__.
2. If I eat too much, I get __full__
3. Last night, I __ate__ too much.

68

Directions: Write the words below. Say them as you write them.

Directions: Write the missing letters from the words below. Use the words from the box to help you.

| most | more | always |

1. mo __s__ t
2. a __l__ way __s__
3. mo __r__ e

Now, write a sentence using one of the words from the box.

__Answers will vary.__

69

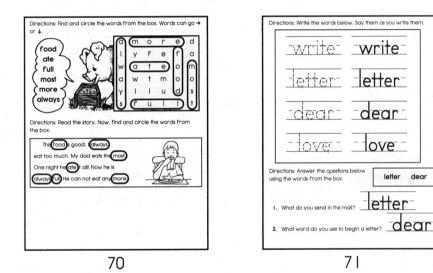

Directions: Find and circle the words from the box. Words can go → or ↓.

Directions: Read the story. Now, find and circle the words from the box.

This food is good. I always eat too much. My dad eats the most. One night he ate it all! Now he is always full. He can not eat any more.

70

Directions: Write the words below. Say them as you write them.

write — write
letter — letter
dear — dear
love — love

Directions: Answer the questions below using the words from the box.

| letter | dear |

1. What do you send in the mail? __letter__
2. What word do you use to begin a letter? __dear__

71

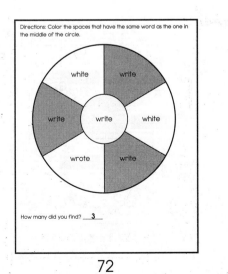

Directions: Color the spaces that have the same word as the one in the middle of the circle.

white, write, write, write, white, wrote, write

How many did you find? __3__

72

Directions: Write the words below. Say them as you write them.

yesterday — yesterday
soon — soon
fine — fine

Directions: Circle the word that is the opposite of the underlined word.

1. I went home _yesterday_. house (today) no
2. The bus will be here _soon_. (later) sun hot
3. We are _fine_. sing song (sick)

Now, write this sentence.
I was fine yesterday.

__I was fine yesterday.__

73

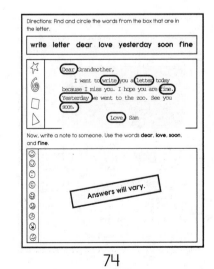

Directions: Find and circle the words from the box that are in the letter.

| write | letter | dear | love | yesterday | soon | fine |

(Dear) Grandmother,
  I want to (write) you a (letter) today because I miss you. I hope you are (fine). (Yesterday) we went to the zoo. See you (soon).
  (Love,) Sam

Now, write a note to someone. Use the words **dear**, **love**, **soon**, and **fine**.

__Answers will vary.__

74

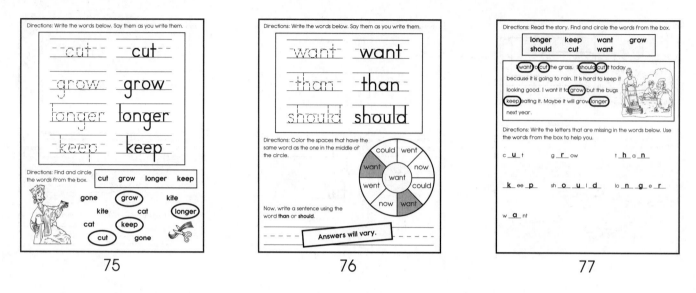

75

76

77

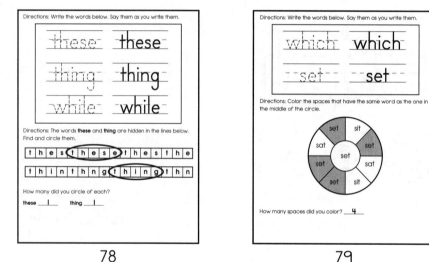

78

79

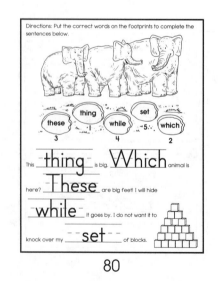

80

81

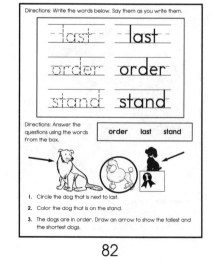

82

Answer Key

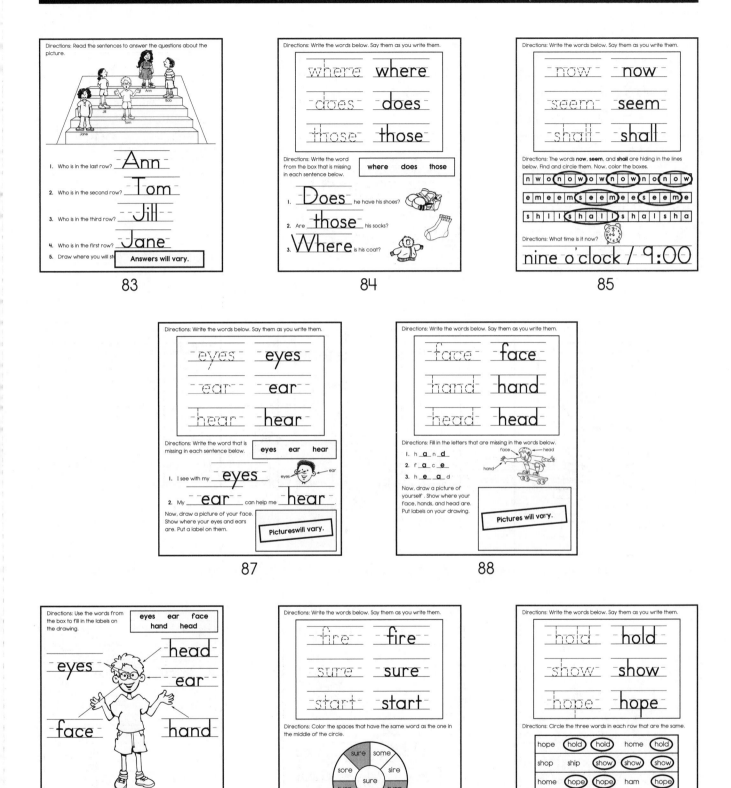

83

84

85

87

88

89

90

91

Answer Key

Page 92

Directions: Read the story. Find and circle the words from the box.

| start | sure | hold | show | hope | fire |

It is cold and time to (start) a (fire). My dad will (show) us how to (start) the (fire). I (hope) it gets warm soon. I will (hold) my hands close to the (fire) to warm up. My dad says, "Be (sure) not to get too close."

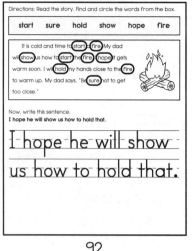

Now, write this sentence.
I hope he will show us how to hold that.

I hope he will show us how to hold that.

92

Page 93

Directions: Write the words below. Say them as you write them.

right — right
left — left
myself — myself

Directions: Read the sentences. Now, follow the directions.
1. Circle the dog on the right.
2. Color the dog on the left.
3. Draw an arrow to the cat on the left.
4. Color the cat on the right.

Now, complete this sentence.

I like myself because

Answers will vary.

93

Page 94

Directions: Write the words below. Say them as you write them.

help — help
small — small
pair — pair

Directions: Draw a line to match the pants that have the same words on them.

| help | small | pair |

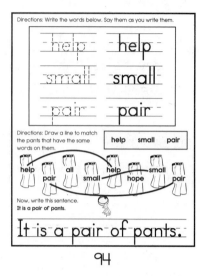

help pair all small help hope small

Now, write this sentence.
It is a pair of pants.

It is a pair of pants.

94

Page 95

Directions: Find and circle the words from the box. Words can go → or ↓.

right
left
myself
help
small
pair

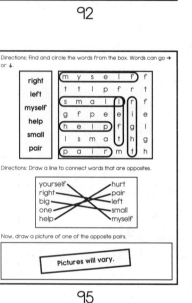

m y s e l f f
t t l p f r t
s m a l l f f
g f p e e i e
h e l p f g l
l s m a t h g
p a i r m t h

Directions: Draw a line to connect words that are opposites.

yourself — hurt
right — pair
big — left
one — small
help — myself

Now, draw a picture of one of the opposite pairs.

Pictures will vary.

95

Page 97

Directions: Write the words below. Say them as you write them.

present — present
bring — bring
sing — sing

Directions: Color the boxes that have **present**, **bring**, and **sing** in them. Use a different color for each word.

song	present	bang	sing
pretty	bring	song	present
sing	present	bright	sang
present	pretty	sing	bring

How many did you find?

present __4__   bring __2__   sing __3__

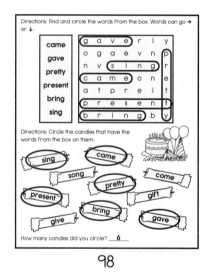

97

Page 98

Directions: Find and circle the words from the box. Words can go → or ↓.

came
gave
pretty
present
bring
sing

g a v e r l y
o g a e v n p
n v s i n g r
c a m e o n e
a t p r e i t
p r e s e n t
b r i n g b

Directions: Circle the candles that have the words from the box on them.

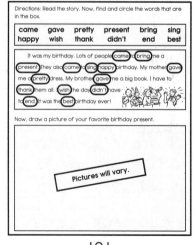

sing came song come pretty present gift bring give gave

How many candles did you circle? __6__

98

Page 99

Directions: Write the words below. Say them as you write them.

happy — happy
wish — wish
thank — thank

Directions: Draw a string to tie the balloons together that have the words from the box on them.

| happy | wish | thank |

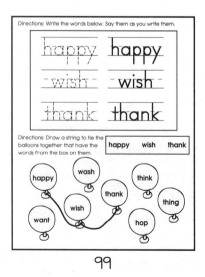

happy wash think thank thing want wish hop

99

Page 100

Directions: Write the words below. Say them as you write them.

didn't — didn't
end — end
best — best

Directions: Color the boxes that have the words **didn't**, **end**, and **best** in them. Use a different color for each word.

don't	end	send	best
send	best	bet	end
end	bend	rest	didn't
best	didn't	did	send

How many did you find?

didn't __2__   end __3__   best __3__

100

Page 101

Directions: Read the story. Now, find and circle the words that are in the box.

| came | gave | pretty | present | bring | sing |
| happy | wish | thank | didn't | end | best |

It was my birthday. Lots of people (came) to (bring) me a (present). They also (came) to (sing) (happy) birthday. My mother (gave) me a (pretty) dress. My brother (gave) me a big book. I have to (thank) them all. I (wish) the day (didn't) have to (end). It was the (best) birthday ever!

Now, draw a picture of your favorite birthday present.

Pictures will vary.

101

Answer Key

Page 102
1. I <u>got</u> a dog.
2. He sleeps in a <u>box</u>.
3. My dog is <u>big</u>.
4. He <u>ran</u> in the yard.
5. I <u>let</u> him lick me.

Page 103
1. The <u>girl</u> had a dog.
2. The dog liked to <u>run</u> away fast.
3. The girl had to <u>find</u> the dog.
4. She had to <u>look</u> for him.
5. Did she find him? <u>Yes</u>, she did!
6. Now the girl wants the dog to <u>sit</u>.

Page 104
1. It is dark at <u>night</u>.
2. I get in my <u>bed</u>.
3. I have to go to <u>sleep</u> now.
4. In the <u>morning</u> I get up.
5. I have to get up <u>early</u>.
6. And I have to go to <u>school</u>.

Page 105
1. I see a <u>door</u>.
2. It is <u>open</u>.
3. Don't <u>close</u> the door.
4. <u>Leave</u> the light on.
5. Please don't turn <u>off</u> the light.
6. I <u>don't</u> like the dark.

Page 106
1. We went for a <u>ride</u>.
2. We drove in the <u>car</u>.
3. The ride <u>took</u> a long time.
4. We went <u>far</u> away.
5. Then we went <u>around</u> the park.
6. At last we came <u>back</u> home.

Page 107
1. I have to <u>wash</u> the dishes.
2. I will <u>carry</u> them to the sink.
3. I need to get some <u>water</u>.
4. The water is not too <u>warm</u>.
5. Now the dishes are <u>clean</u>.
6. Now I am <u>done</u>!

Page 108
1. It is <u>cold</u> outside.
2. I <u>better</u> not go outside yet.
3. My <u>dress</u> is not very warm.
4. First, I need to put on some warm <u>clothes</u>.
5. My mom gives me a warm <u>coat</u>.
6. She is very <u>kind</u> to me.

Page 109
1. The <u>food</u> is good here.
2. I <u>always</u> eat too much.
3. My dad eats the <u>most</u> food.
4. He <u>ate</u> all the food on his plate!
5. Now he is <u>full</u>.
6. He can not eat any <u>more</u>.

Page 110
1. Bob wrote a <u>letter</u> to his sister.
2. He wrote, "<u>Dear</u> Pat, how are you?"
3. "I am <u>fine</u>," Bob wrote.
4. "<u>Yesterday</u> I went to the park."
5. He signed it, "<u>Love</u>, Bob."
6. He will mail it <u>soon</u>.

Page 111
1. I can <u>hear</u> the dog bark.
2. I can hear with my <u>ear</u>.
3. I have two <u>eyes</u>.
4. I can see my <u>face</u> in the mirror.
5. My hat is on my <u>head</u>.
6. A <u>hand</u> has five fingers.

Page 113
May I say this?
He likes to run fast.
She had to look for him.
Can she buy a pencil?

Page 114
A rock is under a tree.
I will leave the car.
Please close the door.
Let's get another pumpkin.

Page 115
That plane can fly fast.
My dad eats the most.
A hand has five fingers.
I will write a letter to you.

Page 116
He hit a home run.
I will write a letter soon.
I can see with my eyes.
It goes right here.